Big Data Now
2013 Edition

O'Reilly Media, Inc.

Beijing · Cambridge · Farnham · Köln · Sebastopol · Tokyo

Big Data Now

by O'Reilly Media, Inc.

Copyright © 2014 O'Reilly Media. All rights reserved.

Printed in the United States of America.

Published by O'Reilly Media, Inc., 1005 Gravenstein Highway North, Sebastopol, CA 95472.

O'Reilly books may be purchased for educational, business, or sales promotional use. Online editions are also available for most titles (*http://my.safaribooksonline.com*). For more information, contact our corporate/institutional sales department: 800-998-9938 or *corporate@oreilly.com*.

Editors: Jenn Webb and Tim O'Brien
Proofreader: Kiel Van Horn

Illustrator: Rebecca Demarest

February 2014:   First Edition

Revision History for the First Edition:

2013-01-22:   First release

Nutshell Handbook, the Nutshell Handbook logo, and the O'Reilly logo are registered trademarks of O'Reilly Media, Inc. *Big Data Now: 2013 Edition* and related trade dress are trademarks of O'Reilly Media, Inc.

Many of the designations used by manufacturers and sellers to distinguish their products are claimed as trademarks. Where those designations appear in this book, and O'Reilly Media, Inc. was aware of a trademark claim, the designations have been printed in caps or initial caps.

While every precaution has been taken in the preparation of this book, the publisher and authors assume no responsibility for errors or omissions, or for damages resulting from the use of the information contained herein.

ISBN: 978-1-449-37420-4

[LSI]

O'REILLY®
Strata
Making Data Work

O'Reilly Strata is the essential source for training and information in data science and big data—with industry news, reports, in-person and online events, and much more.

- Weekly Newsletter
- Industry News & Commentary
- Free Reports
- Webcasts
- Conferences
- Books & Videos

Dive deep into the latest in data science and big data.
strata.oreilly.com

©2013 O'Reilly Media, Inc. The O'Reilly logo is a registered trademark of O'Reilly Media, Inc. 13383

Table of Contents

Introduction. ix

Evolving Tools and Techniques. 1
How Twitter Monitors Millions of Time Series 2
Data Analysis: Just One Component of the Data Science
    Workflow 4
    Tools and Training 5
    The Analytic Lifecycle and Data Engineers 6
Data-Analysis Tools Target Nonexperts 7
    Visual Analysis and Simple Statistics 7
    Statistics and Machine Learning 8
    Notebooks: Unifying Code, Text, and Visuals 9
Big Data and Advertising: In the Trenches 10
    Volume, Velocity, and Variety 11
    Predicting Ad Click-through Rates at Google 11
Tightly Integrated Engines Streamline Big Data Analysis 13
    Interactive Query Analysis: SQL Directly on Hadoop 13
    Graph Processing 14
    Machine Learning 14
    Integrated Engines Are in Their Early Stages 15
Data Scientists Tackle the Analytic Lifecycle 15
    Model Deployment 16
    Model Monitoring and Maintenance 17
    Workflow Manager to Tie It All Together 18
Pattern Detection and Twitter's Streaming API 18
    Systematic Comparison of the Streaming API and the
        Firehose 19
    Identifying Trending Topics on Twitter 20

Moving from Batch to Continuous Computing at Yahoo!	22
Tracking the Progress of Large-Scale Query Engines	24
An open source benchmark from UC Berkeley's Amplab	25
Initial Findings	25
Exploratory SQL Queries	26
Aggregations	26
Joins	27
How Signals, Geometry, and Topology Are Influencing Data Science	28
Compressed Sensing	28
Topological Data Analysis	29
Hamiltonian Monte Carlo	29
Geometry and Data: Manifold Learning and Singular Learning Theory	29
Single Server Systems Can Tackle Big Data	30
One Year Later: Some Single Server Systems that Tackle Big Data	30
Next-Gen SSDs: Narrowing the Gap Between Main Memory and Storage	31
Data Science Tools: Are You "All In" or Do You "Mix and Match"?	32
An Integrated Data Stack Boosts Productivity	32
Multiple Tools and Languages Can Impede Reproducibility and Flow	32
Some Tools that Cover a Range of Data Science Tasks	33
Large-Scale Data Collection and Real-Time Analytics Using Redis	34
Returning Transactions to Distributed Data Stores	37
The Shadow of the CAP Theorem	37
NoSQL Data Modeling	38
Revisiting the CAP Theorem	39
Return to ACID	39
FoundationDB	40
A New Generation of NoSQL	41
Data Science Tools: Fast, Easy to Use, and Scalable	42
Spark Is Attracting Attention	42
SQL Is Alive and Well	42
Business Intelligence Reboot (Again)	42
Scalable Machine Learning and Analytics Are Going to Get Simpler	43
Reproducibility of Data Science Workflows	44

MATLAB, R, and Julia: Languages for Data Analysis	45
MATLAB	45
R	50
Julia	54
…and Python	57
Google's Spanner Is All About Time	58
Meet Spanner	58
Clocks Galore: Armageddon Masters and GPS Clocks	60
"An Atomic Clock Is Not that Expensive"	61
The Evolution of Persistence at Google	61
Enter Megastore	62
Hey, Need Some Continent-Wide ACID? Here's Spanner	63
Did Google Just Prove an Entire Industry Wrong?	63
QFS Improves Performance of Hadoop Filesystem	64
Seven Reasons Why I Like Spark	66
Once You Get Past the Learning Curve … Iterative Programs	67
It's Already Used in Production	68

Changing Definitions. 69

Do You Need a Data Scientist?	70
How Accessible Is Your Data?	70
Another Serving of Data Skepticism	72
A Different Take on Data Skepticism	74
Leading Indicators	76
Data's Missing Ingredient? Rhetoric	78
Data Skepticism	80
On the Importance of Imagination in Data Science	81
Why? Why? Why!	84
Case in Point	85
The Take-Home Message	87
Big Data Is Dead, Long Live Big Data: Thoughts Heading to Strata	87
Keep Your Data Science Efforts from Derailing	89
I. Know Nothing About Thy Data	89
II. Thou Shalt Provide Your Data Scientists with a Single Tool for All Tasks	89
III. Thou Shalt Analyze for Analysis' Sake Only	90
IV. Thou Shalt Compartmentalize Learnings	90
V. Thou Shalt Expect Omnipotence from Data Scientists	90
Your Analytics Talent Pool Is Not Made Up of Misanthropes	90

#1: Analytics Is Not a One-Way Conversation	91
#2: Give Credit Where Credit Is Due	91
#3: Allow Analytics Professionals to Speak	92
#4: Don't Bring in Your Analytics Talent Too Late	92
#5: Allow Your Scientists to Get Creative	93
How Do You Become a Data Scientist? Well, It Depends	93
New Ethics for a New World	97
Why Big Data Is Big: The Digital Nervous System	99
From Exoskeleton to Nervous System	99
Charting the Transition	100
Coming, Ready or Not	101
Follow Up on Big Data and Civil Rights	102
Nobody Notices Offers They Don't Get	102
Context Is Everything	103
Big Data Is the New Printing Press	103
While You Slept Last Night	104
The Veil of Ignorance	104
Three Kinds of Big Data	105
Enterprise BI 2.0	106
Civil Engineering	107
Customer Relationship Optimization	108
Headlong into the Trough	109

Real Data **111**

Finding and Telling Data-Driven Stories in Billions of Tweets	112
"Startups Don't Really Know What They Are at the Beginning"	115
On the Power and Perils of "Preemptive Government"	119
How the World Communicates in 2013	124
Big Data Comes to the Big Screen	127
The Business Singularity	129
Business Has Been About Scale	130
Why Software Changes Businesses	131
It's the Cycle, Stupid	132
Peculiar Businesses	134
Stacks Get Hacked: The Inevitable Rise of Data Warfare	135
Injecting Noise	138
Mistraining the Algorithms	139
Making Other Attacks More Effective	139
Trolling to Polarize	140

The Year of Data Warfare	141
Five Big Data Predictions for 2013	141
Emergence of a big data architecture	142
Hadoop Is Not the Only Fruit	143
Turnkey Big Data Platforms	143
Data Governance Comes into Focus	144
End-to-End Analytic Solutions Emerge	144
Printing Ourselves	145
Software that Keeps an Eye on Grandma	147
In the 2012 Election, Big Data-Driven Analysis and Campaigns Were the Big Winners	149
The Data Campaign	150
Tracking the Data Storm Around Hurricane Sandy	151
Stay Safe, Keep Informed	154
A Grisly Job for Data Scientists	155

Health Care ... 157

Moving to the Open Health-Care Graph	158
Genomics and Privacy at the Crossroads	163
A Very Serious Game That Can Cure the Orphan Diseases	167
Data Sharing Drives Diagnoses and Cures, If We Can Get There (Part 1)	169
An Intense Lesson in Code Sharing	169
Synapse as a Platform	170
Data Sharing Drives Diagnoses and Cures, If We Can Get There (Part 2)	171
Measure Your Words	172
Making Government Health Data Personal Again	173
Driven to Distraction: How Veterans Affairs Uses Monitoring Technology to Help Returning Veterans	177
Growth of SMART Health Care Apps May Be Slow, but Inevitable	179
The Premise and Promise of SMART	180
How Far We've Come	181
Keynotes	182
Did the Conference Promote More Application Development?	183
Quantified Self to Essential Self: Mind and Body as Partners in Health	185

Introduction

Welcome to *Big Data Now 2013*! We pulled together our top posts from late fall 2012 through late fall 2013. The biggest challenge of assembling content for a blog retrospective is timing, and we worked hard to ensure the best and most relevent posts are included. What made the cut? "Timeless" pieces and entries that covered the ways in which big data has evolved over the past 12 months—and that it has. In 2013, "big data" became more than just a technical term for scientists, engineers, and other technologists—the term entered the mainstream on a myriad of fronts, becoming a household word in news, business, health care, and people's personal lives. The term became synonymous with intelligence gathering and spycraft, as reports surfaced of the NSA's reach moving beyond high-level political figures and terrorist organizations into citizens' personal lives. It further entered personal space through doctor's offices as well as through wearable computing, as more and more consumers entered the Quantified Self movement, measuring their steps, heart rates, and other physical behaviors. The term became commonplace on the nightly news and in daily newspapers as well, as journalists covered natural disasters and reported on President Obama's "big data" campaign. These topics and more are covered throughout this retrospective.

Posts have been divided into four main chapters:

Evolving Tools and Techniques
> The community is constantly coming up with new tools and systems to process and manage data at scale. This chapter contains entries that cover trends and changes to the databases, tools, and techniques being used in the industry. At this year's Strata Conference in Santa Clara, one of the tracks was given the title

"Beyond Hadoop." This is one theme of *Big Data Now 2013*, as more companies are moving beyond a singular reliance on Hadoop. There's a new focus on time-series data and how companies can use a different set of technologies to gain more immediate benefits from data as it is collected.

Changing Definitions

Big data is constantly coming under attack by many commentators as being an amorphous marketing term that can be bent to suit anyone's needs. The field is still somewhat "plastic," and new terms and ideas are affecting big data—not just in how we approach the problems to which big data is applied, but in how we think about the people involved in the process. What does it mean to *be* a data scientist? How does one relate to data analysts? What constitutes big data, and how do we grapple with the societal and ethical impacts of a data-driven world? Many of the "big idea" posts of 2013 fall into the category of "changing definitions." Big data is being quenched into a final form, and there is still some debate about what it is and what its effects will be on industry and society.

Real Data

Big data has gone from a term used by technologists to a term freely exchanged on the nightly news. Data at scale—and its benefits and drawbacks—are now a part of the culture. This chapter captures the effects of big data on real-world problems. Whether it is how big data was used to respond to Hurricane Sandy, how the Obama campaign managed to win the presidency with big data, or how data is used to devise novel solutions to real-world problems, this chapter covers it.

Health Care

This chapter takes a look at the intersections of health care, government, privacy, and personal health monitoring. From a sensor device that analyzes data to help veterans to Harvard's SMART platform of health care apps, from the CDC's API to genomics and genetics all the way to the Quantified Self movement, the posts in this section cover big data's increasing role in every aspect of our health care industry.

Evolving Tools and Techniques

If you consider the publishing of Google's "BigTable" paper as an initial event in the big data movement, there's been nine years of development of this space, and much of the innovation has been focused solely on technologies and tool chains. For years, big data was confined to a cloistered group of elite technicians working for companies like Google and Yahoo, and over time big data has worked its way through the industry. Any company that gathers data at a certain scale will have someone somewhere working on a system that makes use of big data, but the databases and tools used to manage data at scale have been constantly evolving.

Four years ago, "big data" meant "Hadoop," and while this is still very much true for a large portion of the Strata audience, there are other components in the big data technology stack that are starting to outshine the fundamental approach to storage that previously had a monopoly on big data. In this chapter, the posts we chose take a look at evolving tools and storage solutions, and at how companies like Twitter and Yahoo! are managing data at scale. You'll also notice that Ben Lorica has a very strong presence. Lorica's Twitter handle—@bigdata—says it all; he's paying so much attention to the industry, his coverage is not only thorough, but insightful and well-informed.

How Twitter Monitors Millions of Time Series

A distributed, near real-time system simplifies the collection, storage, and mining of massive amounts of event data

By Ben Lorica (*http://bit.ly/1dptMRz*)

One of the keys to Twitter's ability to process 500 million tweets daily (*http://bit.ly/1al4lXe*) is a software development process that values monitoring and measurement. A recent post (*http://bit.ly/1dptN8f*) from the company's *Observability* team detailed the software stack for monitoring the performance characteristics of software services and alerting teams when problems occur. The Observability stack collects 170 million individual *metrics* (time series) every minute and serves up 200 million queries per day. Simple query tools are used to populate charts and dashboards (a typical user monitors about 47 charts).

The stack is about three years old[1] and consists of *instrumentation*[2] (data collection primarily via Finagle (*http://bit.ly/1al4p9a*)), *storage* (Apache Cassandra), *a query language* and *execution engine*,[3] *visualization*,[4] and basic *analytics*. Four distinct Cassandra clusters are used to serve different requirements (real-time, historical, aggregate, index). A lot of engineering work went into making these tools as simple to use as possible. The end result is that these different pieces provide a flexible and interactive framework for developers: insert a few lines of (instrumentation) code and start viewing charts within minutes.[5]

---

1. The precursor to the Observability stack was a system that relied on tools like Ganglia (*http://oreil.ly/RLxPPG*) and Nagios (*http://oreil.ly/1dptLgy*).
2. "Just as easy as adding a print statement."
3. In-house tools written in Scala, the queries are written in a "declarative, functional inspired language". In order to achieve near real-time latency, in-memory caching techniques are used.
4. In-house tools based on HTML + Javascript, including command line tools for creating charts and dashboards.
5. The system is best described as near real-time. Or more precisely, human real-time (since humans are still in the loop).

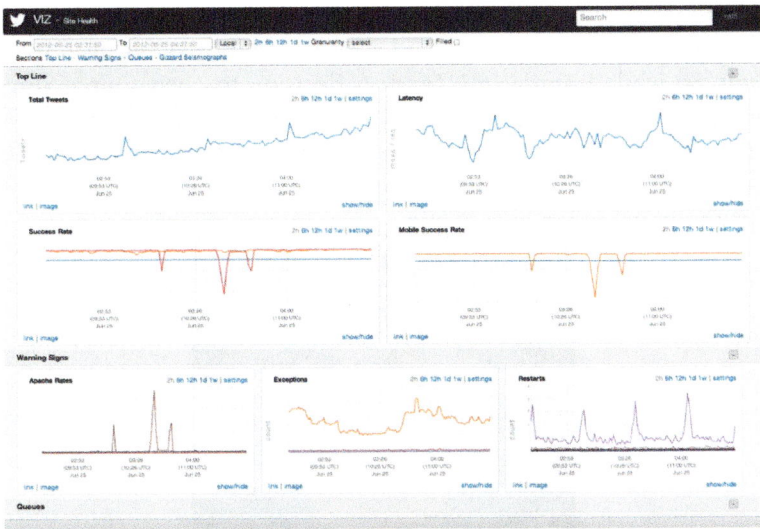

The Observability stack's suite of analytic functions is a work in progress—only simple tools are currently available. Potential anomalies are highlighted visually and users can input simple alerts ("if the value exceeds 100 for 10 minutes, alert me"). While rule-based alerts are useful, they cannot proactively detect unexpected problems (or unknown unknowns) (*http://bit.ly/1dptNVU*). When faced with tracking a large number of time series, correlations are essential: if one time series signals an anomaly, it's critical to know what others we should be worried about. In place of *automatic* correlation detection, for now Observability users leverage Zipkin (*http://bit.ly/1al4nhB*) (a distributed tracing system) to identify service dependencies. But its solid technical architecture should allow the Observability team to easily expand its analytic capabilities. Over the coming months, the team plans to add tools[6] for *pattern matching* (search) as well as automatic correlation and anomaly detection.

While latency requirements tend to grab headlines (e.g., high-frequency trading), Twitter's Observability stack addresses a more common pain point: managing and mining many millions of time series. In an earlier post (*http://bit.ly/1al4ny6*), I noted that many interesting systems developed for monitoring IT operations are begin-

---

6. Dynamic time warping (*http://bit.ly/1dptOsK*) at massive scale is on their radar. Since historical data is archived, simulation tools (for what-if scenario analysis) are possible but currently not planned. In an earlier post I highlighted one such tool from Cloud-Physics (*http://bit.ly/1al4ny6*).

ning to tackle this problem. As self-tracking apps continue to proliferate, massively scalable backend systems for time series need to be built. So while I appreciate Twitter's decision to open source Summingbird (*http://bit.ly/1al4qdh*), I think just as many users will want to get their hands on an open source version of their Observability stack (*http://bit.ly/1dptN8f*). I certainly hope the company decides to open source it in the near future.

Data Analysis: Just One Component of the Data Science Workflow

Specialized tools run the risk of being replaced by others that have more coverage

By Ben Lorica (*http://bit.ly/1dptMRz*)

Judging from articles in the popular press, the term *data scientist* has increasingly come to refer to someone who specializes in data *analysis* (statistics, machine-learning, etc.). This is unfortunate since the term originally described someone who could cut across disciplines. Far from being confined to data analysis, a typical data science workflow[7] means jumping back and forth between a series of interdependent tasks. Data scientists tend to use a variety of tools (*http://bit.ly/1al4rxQ*), often across different programming languages. Workflows that involve many different tools require a lot of context-switching, which affects productivity and impedes reproducability (*http://bit.ly/1dptSbU*).

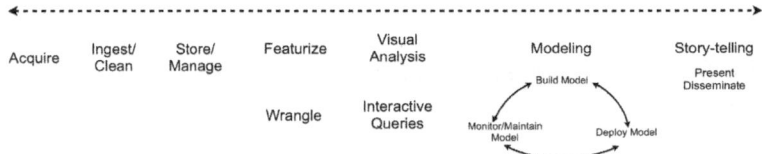

Tools and Training

People who build tools appreciate the value of having their solutions span across the data science workflow. If a tool only addresses a limited section of the workflow, it runs the risk of being replaced by others that have more coverage. Platfora is as proud of its data store (the fractal cache) and data-wrangling[8] tools as of its interactive visualization capabilities. The Berkeley Data Analytics Stack (BDAS) and the Hadoop community are expanding to include analytic engines (*http://bit.ly/1dptSsr*) that increase their coverage—over the next few months BDAS components for machine-learning (MLbase (*http://bit.ly/1al4v0N*)) and graph analytics (GraphX (*http://bit.ly/1dptQRk*)) are slated for their initial release. In an earlier post (*http://bit.ly/1al4sCb*), I highlighted a number of tools that simplify the application of advanced analytics and the interpretation of results (*http://bit.ly/1al4sCb*). Analytic tools are getting to the point that in the near future I expect that many (routine) data analysis tasks will be performed by business analysts and other nonexperts.

The people who train future data scientists also seem aware of the need to teach more than just data *analysis* skills. A quick glance at the syllabi

---

7. For a humorous view, see Data Science skills as a subway map (*http://bit.ly/1dptRF9*).

8. Here's a funny take (*http://bit.ly/1al4utD*) on the rule-of-thumb that data wrangling accounts for 80% of time spent on data projects: "In Data Science, 80% of time spent prepare data, 20% of time spent complain about need for prepare data."

and curricula of a few[9] data science courses and programs reveals that —at least in some training programs—students get to learn other components of the data science workflow. One course that caught my eye: CS 109 at Harvard (*http://bit.ly/1al4zh3*) seems like a nice introduction to the many facets of *practical* data science—plus it uses IPython notebooks (*http://bit.ly/1al4ABA*), Pandas, and scikit-learn (*http://bit.ly/1al4sCb*)!

The Analytic Lifecycle and Data Engineers

As I noted in a recent post (*http://bit.ly/1al4B8u*), model *building* is only one aspect of the analytic lifecycle. Organizations are starting to pay more attention to the equally important tasks of model *deployment*, *monitoring*, and *maintenance* (*http://bit.ly/1al4B8u*). One telling example comes from a recent paper on sponsored search advertising at Google (*http://bit.ly/1al4Bpa*): a simple model was chosen (logistic regression) and most of the effort (and paper) was devoted to devising ways to efficiently train, deploy, and maintain it in production.

In order to deploy their models into production, data scientists learn to work closely with folks who are responsible for building scalable data infrastructures: data *engineers*. If you talk with enough startups in Silicon Valley, you quickly realize that data *engineers* are in even higher[10] demand than data *scientists*. Fortunately, some forward-thinking consulting services are stepping up to help companies address both their data *science* and data *engineering* needs.

---

9. Here is a short list: UW Intro to Data Science (*http://bit.ly/1al4t8W*) and Certificate in Data Science (*http://bit.ly/1dptTwJ*), CS 109 at Harvard (*http://bit.ly/1al4zh3*), Berkeley's Master of Information and Data Science program (*http://bit.ly/1dptUAB*), Columbia's Certification of Professional Achievement in Data Sciences (*http://bit.ly/1al4wBN*), MS in Data Science (*http://bit.ly/1dptV7A*) at NYU, and the Certificate of Advanced Study In Data Science (*http://bit.ly/1al4AkR*) at Syracuse.

10. I'm not sure why the popular press hasn't picked up on this distinction. Maybe it's a testament to the the buzz surrounding data science. See http://medriscoll.com/post/49783223337/let-us-now-praise-data-engineers (*http://bit.ly/1dptYAs*).

Data-Analysis Tools Target Nonexperts

Tools simplify the application of advanced analytics and the interpretation of results

By Ben Lorica (*http://bit.ly/1dptMRz*)

A new set of tools makes it easier to do a variety of data analysis tasks. Some require no programming, while other tools make it easier to combine code, visuals, and text in the same workflow. They enable users who aren't statisticians or data geeks to do data analysis. While most of the focus is on enabling the application of analytics to data sets, some tools also help users with the often tricky task of interpreting results. In the process, users are able to discern patterns and evaluate the value of data sources by themselves, and only call upon expert[11] data analysts when faced with nonroutine problems.

Visual Analysis and Simple Statistics

Three Software as a Service (SaaS) startups—DataHero (*http://bit.ly/1al4BW9*), DataCracker (*http://bit.ly/1dptZ7r*), and Statwing (*http://bit.ly/1al4CcA*)—make it easy to perform simple data wrangling, visual analysis, and statistical analysis. All three (particularly DataCracker) appeal to users who analyze consumer surveys. Statwing (*http://bit.ly/1al4CcA*) and DataHero (*http://bit.ly/1al4EBg*) simplify the creation of pivot tables (*http://bit.ly/1dpu2jJ*)[12] and suggest[13] charts that work well with your data. Statwing users are also able to execute and

---

11. Many routine data analysis tasks will soon be performed by business analysts, using tools that require little to no programming. I've recently noticed that the term data scientist is being increasingly used to refer to folks who specialize in analysis (machine-learning or statistics). With the advent of easy-to-use analysis tools, a data scientist will hopefully once again mean someone who possesses skills that cut across several domains (*http://bit.ly/1dptSbU*).

12. Microsoft PowerPivot (*http://bit.ly/1al4F8i*) allows users to work with large data sets (billion of rows), but as far as I can tell, mostly retains the Excel UI.

13. Users often work with data sets with many variables so "suggesting a few charts" is something that many more visual analysis tools should start doing (*http://bit.ly/1dpu2Ag*) (DataHero (*http://bit.ly/1al4Dx5*) highlights this capability). Yet another feature I wish more visual analysis tools would provide (*http://bit.ly/1dpu2Ag*): novice users would benefit from having brief descriptions of charts they're viewing. This idea comes from playing around with BrailleR (*http://bit.ly/1al4DNC*).

view the results of a few standard statistical tests in plain English (detailed statistical outputs are also available).

Statistics and Machine Learning

BigML (*http://bit.ly/1dpu3nN*) and Datameer's Smart Analytics (*http://bit.ly/1al4E4j*) are examples of recent tools that make it easy for business users to apply machine-learning algorithms to data sets (massive data sets, in the case of Datameer). It makes sense to offload routine data analysis tasks to business analysts and I expect other vendors such as Platfora (*http://bit.ly/1dpu1w9*) and ClearStory (*http://bit.ly/1al4EkO*) to provide similar capabilities in the near future.

In an earlier post (*http://bit.ly/1dptSbU*), I described Skytree Adviser (*http://bit.ly/1al4GZW*), a tool that lets users apply statistics and machine-learning techniques on medium-sized data sets. It provides a GUI that emphasizes *tasks* (cluster, classify, compare, etc.) over algorithms, and produces results that include short explanations of the underlying statistical methods (power users can opt for concise results similar to those produced by standard statistical packages). Users also benefit from not having to choose *optimal* algorithms (Skytree Adviser automatically uses ensembles or finds optimal algorithms). As MLbase (*http://bit.ly/1al4v0N*) matures, it will include a declarative[14] language that will shield users from having to select and code specific algorithms. Once the declarative language is hidden behind a UI, it should feel similar to Skytree Adviser. Furthermore, MLbase implements *distributed* algorithms, so it scales to much larger data sets (terabytes) than Skytree Adviser.

Several commercial databases offer *in-database analytics*—native (possibly distributed) analytic functions that let users perform computations (via SQL) without having to move data to another tool. Along those lines, MADlib is an open source library of scalable analytic functions, currently deployable on Postgres and Greenplum. MADlib includes functions for doing clustering, topic modeling, statistics, and many other tasks.

---

14. The initial version of their declarative language (MQL) and optimizer are slated for release this winter.

Notebooks: Unifying Code, Text, and Visuals

Tools have also gotten better for users who don't mind doing some coding. IPython (*http://bit.ly/1a1kFr4*) notebooks are popular among data scientists who use the Python programming language. By letting you intermingle code, text, and graphics, IPython is a great way to conduct *and* document data analysis projects. In addition, *pydata* ("python data") enthusiasts have access to many open source data science tools, including scikit-learn (*http://bit.ly/1dpu4Im*) (for machine learning) and StatsModels (*http://bit.ly/1al4Kc4*) (for statistics). Both are well documented (scikit-learn has documentation (*http://bit.ly/1dpu5vP*) that other open source projects would envy), making it super easy for users to apply advanced analytic techniques to data sets.

IPython technology isn't tied to Python; other frameworks are beginning to leverage this popular interface (there are early efforts from the GraphLab, Spark (*http://bit.ly/1al4Ksz*), and R (*http://bit.ly/1dpu7Ux*) communities). With a startup (*http://bit.ly/1al4KJh*) focused on further improving its usability (*http://bit.ly/1dpu8b7*), IPython integration and a Python API (*http://bit.ly/1al4IB1*) are the first of many features designed to make GraphLab (*http://bit.ly/1dpu8rz*) accessible to a broader user base.

One language that integrates tightly with IPython is Julia (*http://bit.ly/1al4IRr*)—a high-level, high-performance, dynamic programming language for technical computing. In fact, IJulia (*http://bit.ly/1dpu8I1*) is backed by a full IPython kernel that lets you interact with Julia and build graphical notebooks. In addition, Julia now has many libraries for doing simple to advanced data analysis (to name a few: GLM (*http://bit.ly/1al4J7W*), Distributions (*http://bit.ly/1dpu8YF*), Optim (*http://bit.ly/1al4Jot*), GARCH (*http://bit.ly/1dpu9vu*)). In particular, Julia boasts over 200 packages (*http://bit.ly/1al4JF7*), a package manager (*http://bit.ly/1dpu76U*), active mailing lists (*http://bit.ly/1al4MAQ*), and great tools for working with data (e.g., DataFrames (*http://bit.ly/1dpu7ns*) and read/writedlm (*http://bit.ly/1al4PfU*)). IJulia should help this high-performance programming language reach an even wider audience.

Big Data and Advertising: In the Trenches

Volume, variety, velocity, and a rare peek inside sponsored search advertising at Google

By Ben Lorica (*http://bit.ly/1dptMRz*)

The $35B merger of Omnicom and Publicis (*http://reut.rs/1al4N7G*) put the convergence of big data and advertising[15] in the front pages of business publications. Adtech[16] companies have long been at the forefront of many data technologies, strategies, and techniques. By now, it's well known that many impressive large-scale, realtime-analytics systems in production support[17] advertising. A lot of effort has gone towards accurately predicting and measuring click-through rates, so at least for online advertising, data scientists and data engineers have gone a long way towards addressing[18] the famous *"but we don't know which half"* (*http://bit.ly/1dpudvg*) line.

The industry has its share of problems: privacy and creepiness come to mind, and like other technology sectors adtech has its share of "interesting" patent filings (see, for example, here (*http://1.usa.gov/1al4PMZ*), here (*http://bit.ly/1dpudLH*), here (*http://bit.ly/1al4NEH*)). With so many companies dependent on online advertising, some have lamented the industry's hold[19] on data scientists. But online advertising offers data scientists and data engineers lots of interesting technical problems to work on, many of which involve the deployment (and *creation*) of open source tools for massive amounts of data.

---

15. Much of what I touch on in this post pertains to advertising and/or marketing.
16. VC speak for "advertising technology."
17. This is hardly surprising given that advertising and marketing are the major source of revenue of many internet companies.
18. Advertisers and marketers sometimes speak of the 3 C's: context, content, control.
19. An interesting tidbit: I've come across quite a few former finance quants who are now using their skills in ad analytics. Along the same line, the rise of realtime bidding systems for online display ads (*http://bit.ly/1dpub6C*) has led some ad agencies to set up "trading desks". So is it better for these talented folks to work on Madison Avenue or Wall Street?

Volume, Velocity, and Variety

Advertisers strive to make ads as personalized as possible and many adtech systems are designed to scale to many millions of users. This requires distributed computing chops and a massive computing infrastructure. One of the largest systems in production is Yahoo!'s new continuous computing system (*http://bit.ly/1al4NVe*): a recent overhaul of the company's ad targeting systems. Besides the sheer volume of data it handles (100B events per day), this new system allowed Yahoo! to move from batch to near realtime recommendations.

Along with Google's realtime auction for AdWords (*http://bit.ly/1dpubn5*), there are also realtime bidding (RTB) systems for online *display* ads (*http://bit.ly/1dpub6C*). A growing percentage of online display ads are sold via RTB's and industry analysts predict (*http://reut.rs/1dpuezo*) that TV, radio, and outdoor ads will eventually be available on these platforms. RTBs led Metamarkets (*http://bit.ly/1al4Osj*) to develop Druid, an open source, distributed, column store, optimized for realtime OLAP analysis. While Druid was originally developed to help companies monitor RTBs, it's useful in many other domains (Netflix uses Druid (*http://bit.ly/1dpubUm*) for monitoring its streaming media business).

Advertisers and marketers fine-tune their recommendations and predictive models by gathering data from a wide *variety* of sources. They use data acquisition tools (e.g., HTTP cookies (*http://bit.ly/1al4RnW*)), mine social media, data exhaust (*http://bit.ly/1dpucrg*), and subscribe to data providers. They have also been at the forefront of mining sensor data (primarily geo/temporal data from mobile phones) to provide realtime analytics and recommendations.

Using a variety of data types for analytic models is quite challenging in practice. In order to use data on individual users, a lot has to go into data wrangling tools for cleaning, transforming, normalizing, and featurizing disparate data types. Drawing data from multiple sources requires systems that support a variety of techniques, including NLP, graph processing, and geospatial analysis.

Predicting Ad Click-through Rates at Google

A recent paper (*http://bit.ly/1al4OZp*) provides a rare look inside the analytics systems that powers sponsored search advertising at Google. It's a fascinating glimpse into the types of issues Google's data scientists and data engineers have to grapple with—including realtime serving of models with billions of coefficients!

At these data sizes, a lot of effort goes into choosing algorithms that can scale efficiently and can be trained quickly in an online fashion. They take a well-known model (logistic regression) and devise learning algorithms that meet their deployment[20] criteria (among other things, trained models are replicated to many data centers). They use techniques like regularization (*http://bit.ly/1dpufmU*) to save memory at prediction time, subsampling to reduce the size of training sets, and use fewer bits to encode model coefficients (q2.13 encoding (*http://bit.ly/1al4REE*) instead of 64-bit floating-point values).

One of my favorite sections in the paper lists unsuccessful experiments conducted by the analytics team for sponsored search advertising. They applied a few popular techniques from machine learning, all of which the authors describe as not yielding "significant benefit" in their specific set of problems:

- Feature *bagging*: k models are trained on k overlapping subsets of the feature space, and predictions are based on an average of the models
- Feature vector normalization: input vectors were *normalized* ($x \rightarrow (x/||x||)$) using a variety of different norms
- Feature hashing to reduce RAM
- Randomized "dropout" in training:[21] a technique that often produces promising results in computer vision, didn't yield significant improvements in this setting

---

20. "Because trained models are replicated to many data centers for serving, we are much more concerned with sparsification at serving time rather than during training."

21. As the authors describe it (*http://bit.ly/1al4OZp*): "The main idea is to randomly remove features from input example vectors independently with probability p, and compensate for this by scaling the resulting weight vector by a factor of $(1 - p)$ at test time. This is seen as a form of regularization that emulates bagging over possible feature subsets.

Tightly Integrated Engines Streamline Big Data Analysis

A new set of analytic engines makes the case for convenience over performance

By Ben Lorica (*http://bit.ly/1dptMRz*)

The choice of tools for data science includes[22] factors like scalability, performance, and convenience. A while back I noted that data scientists tended to fall into two camps (*http://bit.ly/1al4rxQ*): those who used an integrated stack, and others who stitched frameworks together. Being able to stick with the same programming language and environment is a definite productivity boost since it requires less setup time and context switching.

More recently, I highlighted (*http://bit.ly/1dptSsr*) the emergence of *composable* analytic engines, that leverage data stored in HDFS (or HBase (*http://bit.ly/1dpugqV*) and Accumulo (*http://bit.ly/1al4Ssd*)). These engines may not be the fastest available, but they scale to data sizes that cover most workloads, and most importantly they can operate on data stored in popular distributed data stores. The fastest and most complete set of algorithms will still come in handy, but I suspect that users will opt for slightly slower[23] but more convenient tools for many *routine* analytic tasks.

Interactive Query Analysis: SQL Directly on Hadoop

Hadoop was originally a batch processing platform but late last year a series of interactive[24] query engines became available—beginning with Impala (*http://bit.ly/1890OWX*) and Shark (*http://bit.ly/1al4VnU*), users now have a range of tools for querying data in Hadoop/HBase/Accumulo, including Phoenix (*http://bit.ly/1dpugHC*), Sqrrl (*http://bit.ly/1al4SZe*), Hadapt (*http://bit.ly/1dpugYb*), and Pivotal-HD (*http://bit.ly/1al4Tff*). These engines tend to be slower than MPP databases: early tests showed that Impala and Shark ran slower than an

---

22. There are many other factors involved including cost, importance of open source, programming language, and maturity (at this point, specialized engines have many more "standard" features).

23. As long as performance difference isn't getting in the way of their productivity.

24. What made things a bit confusing for outsiders is the Hadoop community referring to interactive query analysis, as real-time.

MPP database (*http://bit.ly/1dpukqG*) (AWS Redshift). MPP databases may always be faster, but the Hadoop-based query engines only need to be within range ("good enough") before convenience (and *price per terabyte*) persuades companies to offload many tasks over to them. I also expect these new query engines to improve[25] substantially as they're all still fairly new and many more enhancements are planned.

Graph Processing

Apache Giraph (*http://bit.ly/1al4Wbp*) is one of several BSP-inspired graph-processing frameworks (*http://bit.ly/1dptQRk*) that have come out over the last few years. It runs on top of Hadoop, making it an attractive framework for companies with data in HDFS and who rely on tools within the Hadoop ecosystem. At the recent GraphLab workshop, Avery Ching of Facebook alluded to convenience and familiarity (*http://bit.ly/1al4WIe*) as crucial factors for their heavy use of Giraph. Another example is GraphX, the soon to be released graph-processing component (*http://bit.ly/1dptQRk*) of the BDAS stack (*http://bit.ly/1al4Xfo*). It runs slower than GraphLab (*http://bit.ly/1dpu8rz*) but hopes to find an audience[26] among Spark users.

Machine Learning

With Cloudera ML (*http://bit.ly/1al50Yu*) and its recent acquisition of Myrrix (*http://bit.ly/1dpunTB*), I expect Cloudera will at some point release an advanced analytics library that integrates nicely with CDH (*http://bit.ly/1al51f2*) and its other engines (Impala and Search (*http://bit.ly/1dpumin*)). The first release of MLbase (*http://bit.ly/1al4v0N*), the machine-learning component of BDAS, is scheduled over the next few weeks and is set to include tools for many basic tasks (clustering, classification, regression, and collaborative filtering). I don't expect these tools (MLbase, Mahout) to outperform specialized frameworks like GraphLab (*http://bit.ly/1dpu8rz*), Skytree (*http://bit.ly/*

---

25. Performance gap will narrow over time—many of these engines are less than a year old!
26. As I previously noted (*http://bit.ly/1dptQRk*), the developers of GraphX admit that GraphLab will probably always be faster (*http://bit.ly/1dpulLc*): "We emphasize that it is not our intention to beat PowerGraph in performance. ... We believe that the loss in performance may, in many cases, be ameliorated by the gains in productivity achieved by the GraphX system. ... It is our belief that we can shorten the gap in the near future, while providing a highly usable interactive system for graph data mining and computation."

1al4GZW), H20 (*http://bit.ly/1dpumPo*), or wise.io (*http://bit.ly/1al4YQA*). But having seen how convenient and easy it is to use MLbase from within Spark/Scala, I can see myself turning to it for many routine[27] analyses.

Integrated Engines Are in Their Early Stages

Data in distributed systems like Hadoop can now be analyzed *in situ* using a variety of analytic engines. These engines are fairly new, and performance improvements will narrow the gap with specialized systems. This is good news for data scientists: they can perform preliminary and routine analyses using tightly integrated engines, and use the more specialized systems for the latter stages of the analytic lifecycle (*http://bit.ly/1al4B8u*).

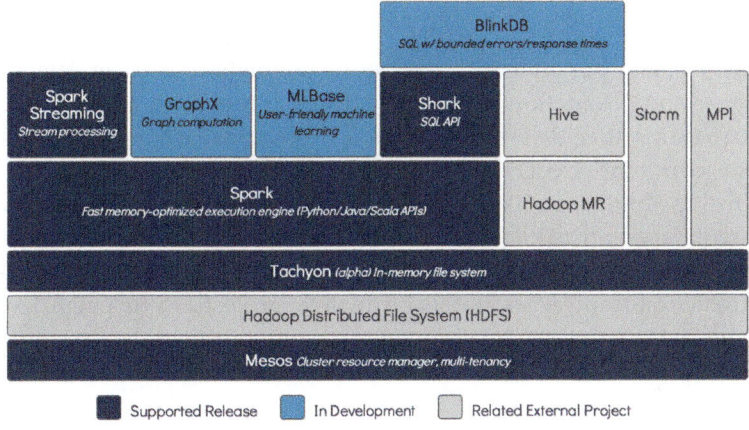

Data Scientists Tackle the Analytic Lifecycle

A new crop of data science tools for deploying, monitoring, and maintaining models

By Ben Lorica (*http://bit.ly/1dptMRz*)

What happens after data scientists build analytic models? Model deployment, monitoring, and maintenance are topics that haven't received as much attention in the past, but I've been hearing more about

---

27. Taking the idea of streamlining a step further, it wouldn't surprise me if we start seeing one of the Hadoop query engines incorporate "in-database" analytics (*http://bit.ly/1dpun5N*).

these subjects from data scientists and software developers. I remember the days when it took weeks before models I built got deployed in production. Long delays haven't entirely disappeared, but I'm encouraged by the discussion and tools that are starting to emerge.

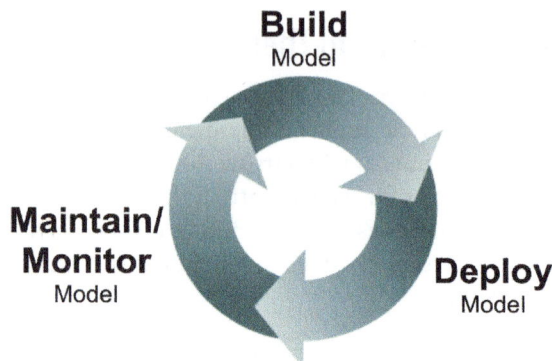

The problem can often be traced to the interaction between data scientists and production engineering teams: if there's a wall separating these teams, then delays are inevitable. In contrast, having data scientists work more closely with production teams makes rapid iteration possible. Companies like LinkedIn, Google, and Twitter work to make sure data scientists know how to interface with their production environment. In many forward-thinking companies, data scientists and production teams work closely on analytic projects. Even a high-level understanding of production environments can help data scientists develop models that are feasible to deploy and maintain.

Model Deployment

Models generally have to be recoded before deployment (e.g., data scientists may favor Python, but production environments may require Java). PMML (*http://bit.ly/17TPl0z*), an XML standard for representing analytic models, has made things easier. Companies who have access to in-database analytics[28] may opt to use their database engines to encode and deploy models.

I've written about open source tools Kiji (*http://bit.ly/1dpugqV*) and Augustus (*http://bit.ly/1al4ZE3*), which consume PMML, let users

---

28. Many commercial vendors offer in-database analytics. The open source library MADlib is another option.

encode models, and take care of model scoring in real-time. In particular the kiji project (*http://bit.ly/1dpuq1z*) has tools for integrating model development (kiji-express (*http://bit.ly/1al55vf*)) and deployment (kiji-scoring (*http://bit.ly/1dpuqP7*)). Built on top of Cascading, Pattern (*http://bit.ly/1al55LM*) is a new framework for building and scoring models on Hadoop (it can also consume PMML).

Quite often models are trained in batch[29] jobs, but the actual scoring is usually easy to do in real time (making it possible for tools like Kiji to serve as *real-time* recommendation engines).

Model Monitoring and Maintenance

When evaluating models, it's essential to measure the right business metrics (modelers tend to favor and obsess over quantitative/statistical measures). With the right metrics and dashboards in place, practices that are routine in IT ops (*http://oreil.ly/1dpusXd*) need to become more common in the analytic space. Already some companies monitor model performance closely—putting in place alerts and processes that let them quickly fix, retrain, or replace models that start tanking.

Prototypes built using historical data can fare poorly when deployed in production, so nothing beats real-world testing. Ideally, the production environment allows for the deployment of multiple (competing) models,[30] in which case tools that let you test and *compare* multiple models are indispensable (via simple A/B tests or even multiarm bandits (*http://oreil.ly/TGaphu*)).

At the recent SAS Global Forum, I came across the SAS Model Manager (*http://bit.ly/1dpurm4*)—a tool that *attempts* to address the analytic lifecycle. Among other things, it lets you store and track versions of models. Proper versioning helps data scientists share their work, but it also can come in handy in other ways. For example, there's a lot of metadata that you can attach to individual models (data schema,

---

29. In certain situations, online learning might be a requirement. In which case, you have to guard against "spam" (garbage in, garbage out).

30. A "model" could be a combination or ensemble of algorithms that reference different features and libraries. It would be nice to have an environment where you can test different combinations of algorithms, features, and libraries.

data lineage, parameters, algorithm(s), code/executable, etc.), all of which are important for troubleshooting[31] when things go wrong.[32]

Workflow Manager to Tie It All Together

Workflow tools provide a good framework for tying together various parts of the analytic lifecycle (SAS Model Manager is used in conjunction with SAS Workflow Studio). They make it easier to reproduce complex analytic projects easier and for team members to collaborate. Chronos (*http://bit.ly/1al56iY*) already lets business analysts piece together complex data-processing pipelines, while analytic tools like the SPSS Modeler (*http://ibm.co/1dpurCw*) and Alpine Data labs (*http://bit.ly/1al56PU*) do the same for machine learning and statistical models.

With companies wanting to unlock the value of big data, there is growing interest in tools for managing the entire analytic lifecycle. I'll close by once again (*http://bit.ly/1dpurTf*) citing one of my favorite quotes[33] on this topic:[34]

> The next breakthrough in data analysis may not be in individual algorithms, but in the ability to rapidly combine, deploy, and maintain existing algorithms. Hazy: Making it Easier to Build and Maintain Big-data Analytics

Pattern Detection and Twitter's Streaming API

In some key use cases, a random sample of tweets can capture important patterns and trends

By Ben Lorica (*http://bit.ly/1dptMRz*)

Researchers and companies who need social media data frequently turn to Twitter's API (*http://bit.ly/1a1kSKQ*) to access a random sample of tweets. Those who can afford to pay (or have been granted access) use the more comprehensive feed (the *firehose*) available through

---

31. Metadata is important for other things besides troubleshooting: it comes in handy for auditing purposes, or when you're considering reusing an older model.
32. A common problem is a schema change may affect whether or not an important feature is getting picked up by a model.
33. Courtesy of Chris Re (*http://stanford.io/1al57n3*) and his students
34. http://queue.acm.org/detail.cfm?id=2431055 (*http://bit.ly/1dpuu1k*)

a group of certified data resellers (*http://bit.ly/1al57TV*). Does the random sample of tweets allow you to capture important patterns and trends? I recently came across two papers that shed light on this question.

Systematic Comparison of the Streaming API and the Firehose

A recent paper from ASU and CMU (*http://bit.ly/1dpuuyg*) compared data from the streaming API and the firehose, and found mixed results. Let me highlight two cases addressed in the paper: identifying popular hashtags and influential users.

Of interest to many users is the list of top hashtags. Can one identify the top n hashtags using data made available through the streaming API? The graph below is a comparison of the streaming API to the firehose: n (as in top n hashtags) versus correlation (Kendall's tau (*http://bit.ly/1al5b67*)). The researchers found that the streaming API provides a good list of hashtags when n is large, but is misleading for small n.

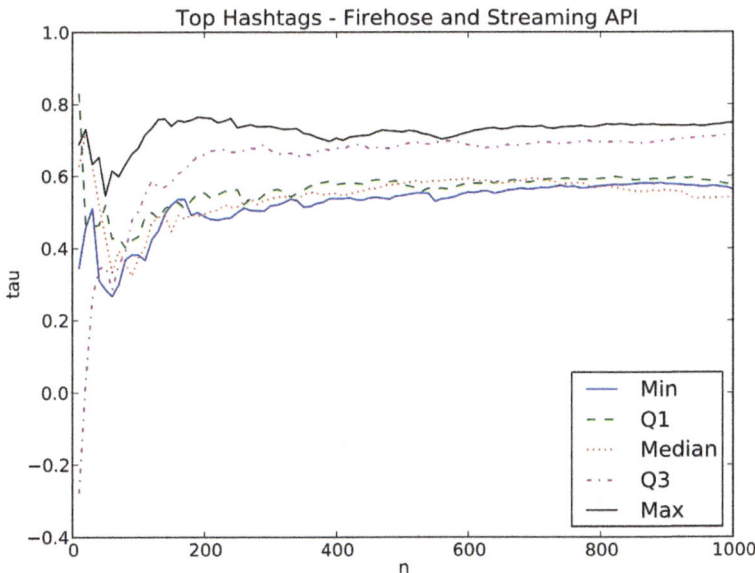

Another area of interest is identifying influential users. The study found that one can identify a *majority* of the most important users just from data available through the streaming API. More precisely,[35] the researchers could identify anywhere from "50%–60% of the top 100 key-players when creating the networks based on one day of streaming API data."

Identifying Trending Topics on Twitter

When people describe Twitter as a source of "breaking news," they're referring to the list[36] of trending topics it produces. A spot on that list is highly coveted[37], and social media marketers mount campaigns designed to secure a place on it. The algorithm for how trending topics were identified was shrouded in mystery (http://n.pr/1al58HC) up until early this year, when a blog post (http://bit.ly/1dpuyhF) (announcing the release of a new search app) hinted at how Twitter identifies trends:

> Our approach to compute the burstiness of image and news facets is an extension of original work by Jon Kleinberg (http://bit.ly/1al58Y8) on bursty structure detection, which is in essence matching current level of burst to one of a predefined set of bursty states, while minimizing too diverse a change in matched states for smooth estimation.

I recently came across (http://bit.ly/1dpuyhF) an interesting *data-driven* (nonparametric) method for identifying trending topics on Twitter (http://bit.ly/1al59eG). It works like a "weighted majority vote k -nearest-neighbors," and uses a set of reference signals (a collection of some topics that trended and some that did not) to compare against.

---

35. For their tests, the researchers assembled graphs whose nodes were comprised of users who tweeted or who were retweeted over given time periods. They measured influence using different notions of centrality (http://bit.ly/1dpuv5p).

36. As with any successful top *n* list, once it takes off, spammers take notice (http://bit.ly/1al5b6n).

37. A 2011 study (http://bit.ly/1dpuvm2) from HP Labs examined what kinds of topics end up on this coveted list (turns out two common sources are retweets of stories from influential stories and new hashtags).

Classification by Experts

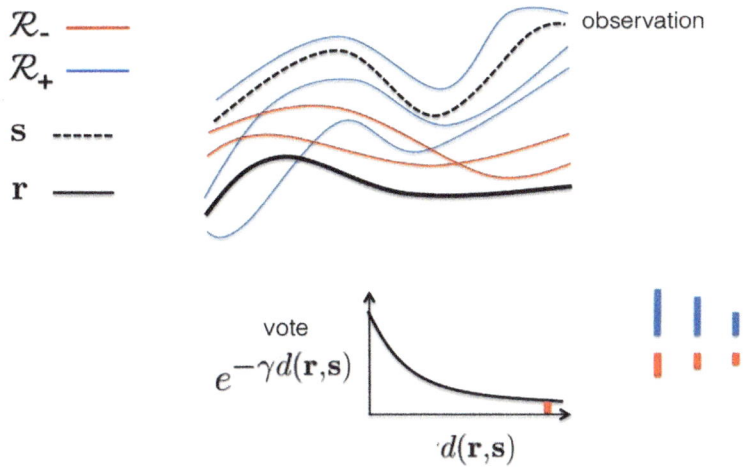

In order to test their new trend-spotting technique, the MIT researchers used data similar[38] to what's available on the Twitter API. Their method produced impressive results: 95% true positive rate (4% false positive), and in 79% of the cases they detected trending topics more than an hour prior to their appearance on Twitter's list.

The researchers were up against a *black box* (Twitter's precise algorithm) yet managed to produce a technique that appears more prescient. As Twimpact (*http://bit.ly/1al5cqS*) co-founder Mikio Braun (*http://bit.ly/1dpuz5a*) pointed out in a tweet (*http://bit.ly/1al5a26*), in essence we have two methods for identifying trends: the official (parametric) model used by Twitter, being estimated by a new (nonparametric) model introduced by the team from MIT!

---

38. From Stanislav Nikolov's master's thesis (*http://bit.ly/1dpuxdm*): "We obtained all data directly from Twitter via the MIT VI-A thesis program. However, the type as well as the amount of data we have used is all publicly available via the Twitter API."

Moving from Batch to Continuous Computing at Yahoo!

Spark, Storm, HBase, and YARN power large-scale, real-time models

Ben Lorica (*http://bit.ly/1dptMRz*)

My favorite session at the recent Hadoop Summit (*http://bit.ly/1al5aiP*) was a keynote by Bruno Fernandez-Ruiz (*http://bit.ly/1dpuzSE*), senior fellow and VP platforms at Yahoo! He gave a nice overview (*http://bit.ly/1al5gaa*) of their analytic and data-processing stack, and shared some interesting factoids about the scale of their big data systems. Notably, many of their production systems now run on MapReduce 2.0 (MRv2) or YARN (*http://bit.ly/1dpuA9h*)—a resource manager that lets multiple frameworks share the same cluster.

Yahoo! was the first company to embrace Hadoop in a big way, and it remains a trendsetter within the Hadoop ecosystem. In the early days, the company used Hadoop for large-scale batch processing (the key example: computing their web index for search). More recently, many of its big data models require low latency alternatives to Hadoop MapReduce. In particular, Yahoo! leverages user and event data to power its targeting, personalization, and other real-time analytic systems. *Continuous Computing* (*http://bit.ly/1al5gGV*) is a term Yahoo! uses to refer to systems that perform computations over small batches of data (over short time windows) in between traditional batch computations that still use Hadoop MapReduce. The goal is to be able to quickly move from raw data, to information, to knowledge.

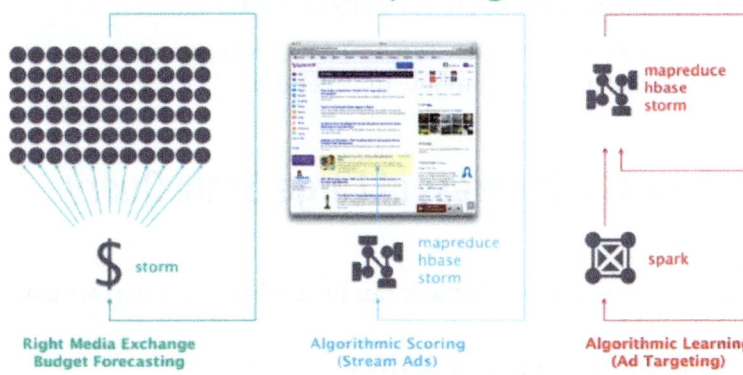

On a side note: many organizations are beginning to use *cluster managers* that let multiple frameworks share the same cluster. In particular, I'm seeing many companies—notably Twitter (*http://wrd.cm/1dpuApO*)—use Apache Mesos (*http://bit.ly/1al5eiu*)[39] (instead of YARN) to run similar services (Storm, Spark, Hadoop MapReduce, HBase) on the same cluster.

Going back to Bruno's presentation, here are some interesting bits—current big data systems at Yahoo! by the numbers:

- 100 billion *events* (clicks, impressions, email content and metadata, etc.) are collected daily, across all of the company's systems.

- A subset of collected events gets passed to a stream processing engine over a Hadoop/YARN cluster: 133,000 events/second are processed, using Storm-on-Yarn (*http://yhoo.it/1dpuC0L*) across 320 nodes. This involves roughly 500 processors and 12,000 threads.

- Iterative computations are performed with Spark-on-YARN, across 40 nodes.

- Sparse data store: 2 PBs of data stored in HBase, across 1,900 nodes. I believe this is one of the largest HBase deployments in production.

---

39. I first wrote about Mesos over two years ago (*http://bit.ly/1dpuAGj*), when I learned that Twitter was using it heavily (*http://bit.ly/1al5huB*). Since then many other companies have deployed Mesos in production, including Twitter, AirBnb, Conviva, UC Berkeley, UC San Francisco, and a slew of startups that I've talked with.

- 8,365 PBs of available raw storage on HDFS, spread across 30,000 nodes (about 150 PBs are currently utilized).
- About 400,000 jobs a day run on YARN, corresponding to about 10,000,000 hours of compute time per day.

Tracking the Progress of Large-Scale Query Engines

A new, open source benchmark can be used to track performance improvements over time

By Ben Lorica (http://bit.ly/1dptMRz)

As organizations continue to accumulate data, there has been renewed interest in *interactive* query engines that scale to terabytes (even petabytes) of data. Traditional MPP databases remain in the mix, but other options are attracting interest. For example, companies willing to upload data into the cloud are beginning to explore Amazon Redshift (http://amzn.to/1dpuE8U)[40], Google BigQuery (http://bit.ly/1dpuCxT), and Qubole (http://bit.ly/1al5f66).

A variety of analytic engines[41] built for Hadoop are allowing companies to bring its low-cost, scale-out architecture to a wider audience. In particular, companies are rediscovering that SQL makes data accessible to lots of users, and many prefer[42] not having to move data to a separate (MPP) cluster. There are many new tools that seek to provide an interactive SQL interface to Hadoop, including Cloudera's Impala (http://bit.ly/1890OWX), Shark (http://bit.ly/1al5ldQ), Hadapt (http://bit.ly/1dpugYb), CitusDB (http://bit.ly/1al5j5Q), Pivotal-HD

---

40. Airbnb has been using Redshift (http://bit.ly/1al5i1D) since early this year.

41. Including some for interactive SQL analysis, machine-learning, streaming, and graphs (http://bit.ly/1dptQRk).

42. The recent focus on Hadoop query engines varies from company to company. Here's an excerpt from a recent interview with Hortonworks CEO Robb Bearden (http://zd.net/1al5fCY): Bearden's take is that real time processing is many years away if ever. "I'd emphasize 'if ever,'" he said. "We don't view Hadoop being storage, processing of unstructured data and real time." Other companies behind distributions, notably Cloudera, see real-time processing as important. "Why recreate the wheel," asks Bearden. Although trying to upend the likes of IBM, Teradata, Oracle and other data warehousing players may be interesting, it's unlikely that a small fry could compete. "I'd rather have my distro adopted and integrated seamlessly into their environment," said Bearden.

(*http://bit.ly/1dpuFtz*), PolyBase (*http://bit.ly/1al5lKY*),[43] and SQL-H (*http://bit.ly/1al5mP4*).

An open source benchmark from UC Berkeley's Amplab

A benchmark (*http://bit.ly/1dpuHBM*) for tracking the progress[44] of scalable query engines has just been released. It's a worthy first effort, and its creators (*http://bit.ly/1al5kXr*) hope to grow the list of tools to include other open source (Drill (*http://bit.ly/1dpuJte*), Stinger (*http://bit.ly/1al5nCC*)) and commercial[45] systems. As these query engines mature and features are added, data from this benchmark can provide a quick synopsis of performance improvements over time.

The initial release includes Redshift, Hive, Impala, and Shark (Hive, Impala, Shark were configured to run on Amazon Web Services (*http://amzn.to/1dpuJJT*)). Hive 0.10 and the most recent versions[46] of Impala and Shark were used (Hive 0.11 was released in mid-May (*http://bit.ly/1al5oq2*) and has not yet been included). Data came from Intel's Hadoop Benchmark Suite (*http://bit.ly/1dpuKgJ*) and CommonCrawl (*http://bit.ly/1a1oM6A*). In the case of Hive/Impala/Shark, data was stored in compressed SequenceFile format using CDH 4.2.0.

Initial Findings

At least for the queries included in the benchmark, Redshift is about 2–3 times faster than Shark(on disk), and 0.3–2 times faster than Shark (in memory). Given that it's built on top of a general purpose engine (Spark), it's encouraging that Shark's performance is within range of

---

43. A recent paper describes PolyBase in detail (*http://bit.ly/1dpuG0o*). Also see Hadapt co-founder, Daniel Abadi's description of how PolyBase and Hadapt differ (*http://bit.ly/1al5kqb*). (Update, 6/6/2013: Dave Dewitt of Microsoft Research, on the design of PolyBase (*http://bit.ly/1dpuG0F*).)

44. To thoroughly *compare* different systems, a generic benchmark such as the one just released, won't suffice. Users still need to load their own data and simulate their workloads.

45. If their terms-of-service allow for inclusion into benchmarks.

46. Versions used: Shark (v0.8 preview, 5/2013); Impala (v1.0, 4/2013); Hive (v0.10, 1/2013)

MPP databases[47] (such as Redshift) that are highly optimized for interactive SQL queries. With new frameworks like Shark and Impala providing speedups *comparable* to those observed in MPP databases, organizations now have the option of using a single system (Hadoop/Spark) instead of two (Hadoop/Spark + MPP database).

Let's look at some of the results in detail in the following sections.

Exploratory SQL Queries

This test involves scanning and filtering operations on progressively larger data sets. Not surprisingly, the fastest results came when Impala and Shark[48] could fit data in-memory. For the largest data set (Query 1C), Redshift is about 2 times faster than Shark (on disk) and 9 times faster than Impala (on disk).

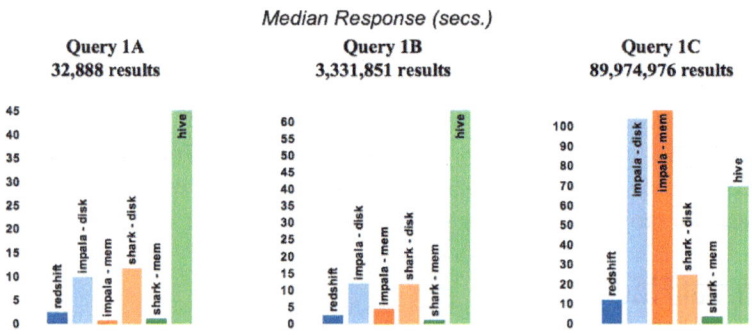

Query: SELECT pageURL, pageRank FROM rankings WHERE pageRank > X

> … As the result sets get larger, Impala becomes bottlenecked on the ability to persist the results back to disk. It seems as if writing large tables is not yet optimized in Impala, presumably because its core focus is business intelligence style queries.

Aggregations

This test involves string parsing and aggregation (where the number of groups progressively gets larger). Focusing on results for the largest

---

47. Being close to MPP database speed is consistent with previous tests (*http://bit.ly/1al5ldQ*) conducted by the Shark team.

48. As I noted in a recent tweet (*http://bit.ly/1al5rlF*) and post (*http://bit.ly/1dpuLRW*): the keys to the BDAS stack (*http://bit.ly/1al4Xfo*) are the use of memory (instead of disk), the use of recomputation (instead of replication) to achieve fault-tolerance, data co-partitioning, and in the case of Shark, the use of column stores.

data set (Query 2C), Redshift is 3 times faster than Shark (on disk) and 6 times faster than Impala (on disk).

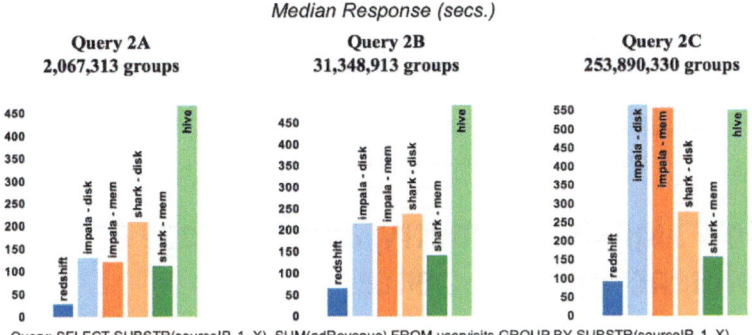

Query: SELECT SUBSTR(sourceIP, 1, X), SUM(adRevenue) FROM uservisits GROUP BY SUBSTR(sourceIP, 1, X)

… Redshift's columnar storage provides greater benefit … since several columns of the UserVisits table are unused. While Shark's in-memory tables are also columnar, it is bottlenecked here on the speed at which it evaluates the SUBSTR expression. Since Impala is reading from the OS buffer cache, it must read and decompress entire rows. Unlike Shark, however, Impala evaluates this expression using very efficient compiled code. These two factors offset each other and Impala and Shark achieve roughly the same raw throughput for in-memory tables. For larger result sets, Impala again sees high latency due to the speed of materializing output tables.

Joins

This test involves merging[49] a large table with a smaller one. Focusing on results for the largest data set (Query 3C), Redshift is 3 times faster than Shark (on disk) and 2 times faster than Impala (on disk).

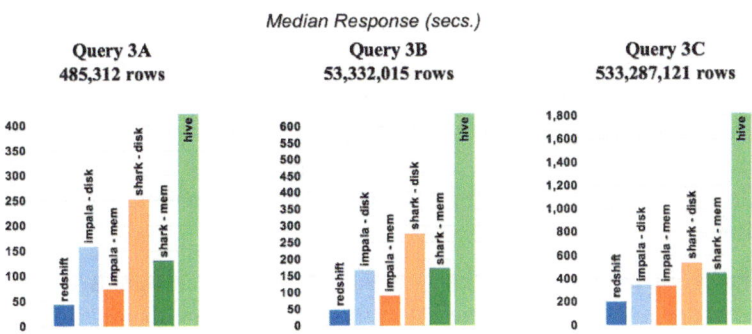

49. The query involves a subquery (http://bit.ly/1dpuM8t) in the FROM clause.

When the join is small (3A), all frameworks spend the majority of time scanning the large table and performing date comparisons. For larger joins, the initial scan becomes a less significant fraction of overall response time. For this reason, the gap between in-memory and on-disk representations diminishes in query 3C. All frameworks perform partitioned joins to answer this query. CPU (due to hashing join keys) and network IO (due to shuffling data) are the primary bottlenecks. Redshift has an edge in this case because the overall network capacity in the cluster is higher.

How Signals, Geometry, and Topology Are Influencing Data Science

Areas concerned with shapes, invariants, and dynamics, in high-dimensions, are proving useful in data analysis

By Ben Lorica (*http://bit.ly/1dptMRz*)

I've been noticing unlikely areas of mathematics pop up in data analysis. While signal processing is a natural fit, topology, differential, and algebraic geometry aren't exactly areas you associate with data science. But upon further reflection perhaps it shouldn't be so surprising that areas that deal in shapes, invariants, and dynamics, in high-dimensions, would have something to contribute to the analysis of large data sets. Without further ado, here are a few examples that stood out for me.

Compressed Sensing

Compressed sensing (*http://bit.ly/1dpuOgu*) is a signal-processing technique that makes efficient data collection possible. As an example, using compressed sensing, images can be reconstructed from small amounts of data. *Idealized sampling* is used to collect information to measure the most important components. By vastly decreasing the number of measurements to be collected, less data needs to stored, and one reduces the amount of time and energy[50] needed to collect signals. Already there have been applications in medical imaging and mobile phones.

The problem is you don't know ahead of time which signals/components are important. A series of numerical experiments led Emanuel Candes to believe (*http://wrd.cm/1al5q1c*) that random samples may

---

50. This leads to longer battery life.

be the answer. The theoretical foundation as to why a random set of signals would work were laid down in a series of papers by Candes and Fields Medalist Terence Tao (*http://bit.ly/1dpuOx4*).[51]

Topological Data Analysis

Tools from *topology*, the mathematics of shapes and spaces, have been generalized to *point clouds of data* (random samples from distributions inside high-dimensional spaces). Topological data analysis (*http://bit.ly/1dpuOND*) is particularly useful for exploratory (visual) data analysis (*http://bit.ly/1dpu2Ag*). Start-up Ayasdi (*http://bit.ly/1dpuNsT*) uses topological data analysis to help business users detect patterns in high-dimensional data sets.

Hamiltonian Monte Carlo

Inspired by ideas from differential geometry and classical mechanics, Hamiltonian Monte Carlo (*http://bit.ly/1al5tKd*) (HMC) is an efficient alternative to popular approximation techniques like Gibbs sampling (*http://bit.ly/1dpuPkI*). A new open source (*http://bit.ly/1al5u0R*) software package called Stan (*http://bit.ly/1dpuNZY*) lets you fit Bayesian statistical models using HMC. (RStan lets you use Stan from within R.)

Geometry and Data: Manifold Learning and Singular Learning Theory

Starting with a set of points in high-dimensional space, manifold learning[52] uses ideas from differential geometry to do dimension reduction (*http://bit.ly/1dpuRci*)—a step often used as a precursor to applying machine-learning algorithms. Singular learning theory (*http://bit.ly/1al5xcX*) draws from techniques in algebraic geometry to generalize the Bayesian Information Criterion (BIC) (*http://bit.ly/1dpuRJ7*) to a much wider set of models. (BIC is a model selection criterion used in machine-learning and statistics.)

---

51. The proofs are complex but *geometric* intuition can be used to explain some of the key ideas, as explained in Tao's "Ostrowski Lecture: The Uniform Uncertainty Principle and Compressed Sensing" (*http://bit.ly/1al5sGi*).

52. I encountered another strand of manifold learning, used for semi-supervised learning (*http://bit.ly/1al5wpw*) in a beautiful talk (*http://bit.ly/1dpuQVH*) by the late Partha Niyogi (*http://bit.ly/1al5wWs*).

Single Server Systems Can Tackle Big Data

Business intelligence, machine-learning, and graph-processing systems tackle large data sets with single servers

By Ben Lorica (http://bit.ly/1dptMRz)

About a year ago, a blog post from SAP (http://bit.ly/1dpuQFe) posited[53] that when it comes to analytics, most companies are in the multiterabyte range: data sizes that are well within the scope of *distributed* in-memory solutions (http://oreil.ly/1dpuSgp) like Spark (http://bit.ly/1al5yh8), SAP HANA (http://bit.ly/1dpuU7L), ScaleOut Software (http://bit.ly/1al5zlh), GridGain (http://bit.ly/1dpuUoh), and Terracotta (http://bit.ly/1al5zBL).

Around the same time, a team of researchers from Microsoft went a step further. They released a study that concluded (http://bit.ly/1dpuTkc) that for many data-processing tasks, scaling by using single machines with very large memories is more efficient than using clusters. They found two clusters devoted to analytics (one at Yahoo! and another at Microsoft) had median job input sizes under 14 GB, while 90% of jobs on a Facebook cluster had input sizes under 100 GB. In addition, the researchers noted that:

> ... for workloads that are processing multi-gigabytes rather than terabyte+ scale, a big-memory server may well provide better performance per dollar than a cluster.

One Year Later: Some Single Server Systems that Tackle Big Data

Business intelligence company SiSense (http://bit.ly/1al5C0n) won the Strata Startup Showcase audience award with Prism—a 64-bit software system that can handle a terabyte of data on a machine with only 8 GB of RAM. Prism[54] relies on disk for storage, moves data to memory when needed, and also takes advantage of the CPU (http://bit.ly/1dpuTkv) (L1/L2/L3 cache). It also comes with a column store and visualization tools that let it easily scale to a hundred terabytes.

---

53. SAP blog post (http://bit.ly/1dpuQFe): "Even with rapid growth of data, 95% of enterprises use between 0.5TB–40 TB of data today."

54. Prism uses a hierarchy (http://bit.ly/1dpuTkv): Accessing data from CPU is faster compared to main memory, which in turn is faster than accessing it from disk.

Late last year I wrote about GraphChi (*http://bit.ly/1dpuUVo*), a graph-processing system that can process graphs with billions of edges with a laptop. It uses a technique called parallel sliding windows to process edges efficiently from disk. GraphChi is part of GraphLab (*http://bit.ly/1dpu8rz*), an open source project that comes with toolkits for collaborative filtering,[55] topic models, and graph processing.

Cassovary (*http://bit.ly/1dpuWN8*) is an open source graph-processing system from Twitter. It's designed to tackle graphs that fit in the memory of a single machine—nevertheless, its creators believe that the use of space-efficient data structures makes it a viable system for "most practical graphs." In fact, it already powers a system familiar to most Twitter users (*http://stanford.io/1al5Dl2*): *WTF* (who to follow) is a recommendation service that suggests users with shared interests and common connections.

Next-Gen SSDs: Narrowing the Gap Between Main Memory and Storage

GraphChi and SiSense scale to large data sets by using disk as primary storage. They speed up performance using techniques that rely on hardware optimization (SiSense) or sliding windows (GraphChi). As part of our investigation into in-memory data management systems (*http://oreil.ly/1dpuSgp*), the potential of next-generation solid state drives (SSDs) (*http://bit.ly/1al5DBz*) has come to our attention. If they live up to the promise of having speeds close to main memory, many more single-server systems for processing and analyzing big data will emerge.

---

55. GraphLab's well-regarded collaborative filtering library has been ported to GraphChi (*http://bit.ly/1al5D4l*).

Data Science Tools: Are You "All In" or Do You "Mix and Match"?

It helps to reduce context switching during long data science workflows

By Ben Lorica (*http://bit.ly/1dptMRz*)

An Integrated Data Stack Boosts Productivity

As I noted in my previous post, Python programmers willing to go "all in" have *Python* tools to cover most of data science (*http://bit.ly/1al4ZE3*). Lest I be accused of oversimplification, a Python programmer still needs to commit to learning a nontrivial set of tools[56]. I suspect that once they invest the time to learn the Python data stack, they tend to stick with it unless they absolutely have to use something else. But being able to stick with the same programming language and environment is a definite productivity boost. It requires less setup time in order to explore data using different *techniques* (viz, stats, ML).

Multiple Tools and Languages Can Impede Reproducibility and Flow

On the other end of the spectrum are data scientists who mix and match tools (*http://bit.ly/1dpuXR0*), and use packages and frameworks from several languages. Depending on the task, data scientists can avail of tools that are scalable, performant, require less[57] code, and contain a lot of features. On the other hand, this approach requires a lot more context-switching, and extra effort is needed to annotate long workflows. Failure to document things properly makes it tough to

---

56. This usually includes matplotlib or Bokeh, Scikit-learn, Pandas, SciPy, and NumPy. But as a general purpose language, you can even use it for data acquisition (e.g. web crawlers or web services).

57. An example would be using R for viz or stats.

reproduce[58] analysis projects, and impedes knowledge transfer[59] within a team of data scientists. Frequent context switching also makes it more difficult to be in a *state of flow* (*http://bit.ly/1dpuZsg*), as one has to think about implementation/package details instead of exploring data. It can be harder to discover interesting stories with your data if you're constantly having to think about what you're doing. (It's still possible, you just have to concentrate a bit harder.)

Some Tools that Cover a Range of Data Science Tasks

More tools that integrate different data science tasks (*http://bit.ly/1dptSbU*) are starting to appear. SAS (*http://bit.ly/1dpuYob*) has long provided tools for data management and wrangling, business intelligence, visualization, statistics, and machine learning. For massive[60] data sets, a new alternative to SAS is ScaleR (*http://bit.ly/1al5Fcp*) from Revolution Analytics. Within ScaleR, programmers use R for data wrangling (rxDataStep (*http://bit.ly/1dpuZZj*)), data visualization (basic viz functions for big data (*http://bit.ly/1al5HRJ*)), and statistical analysis (it comes with a variety of scalable statistical algorithms (*http://bit.ly/1al5Fcp*)).

Startup Alpine Data Labs (*http://bit.ly/1al56PU*) lets users connect to a variety of data sources, manage their data science workflows, and access a limited set of advanced algorithms. Upstart BI vendors Datameer (*http://bit.ly/1dpv0wc*) and Platfora (*http://bit.ly/1dpu1w9*) provide data wrangling and visualization tools. Datameer also provides easy data integration (*http://bit.ly/1dpv2nR*) to a variety of structured/unstructured data sources, analytic functions (*http://bit.ly/1al5IVL*), and PMML to execute predictive analytics (*http://bit.ly/1dpv13s*). The release of MLbase this summer (*http://bit.ly/1al4v0N*) adds machine-learning to the BDAS/Spark (*http://bit.ly/1al5yh8*)

---

58. This pertains to all data scientists, but is *particularly* important to those among us who use a wide variety of tools. Unless you document things properly, when you're using many different tools the results of *very recent* analysis projects can be hard to redo.

59. Regardless of the tools you use, everything starts with knowing something about the *lineage and provenance* of your dataset—something Loom (*http://bit.ly/1al5H45*) attempts to address.

60. A quick and fun tool for exploring smaller data sets is the just released SkyTree Adviser. After users perform data processing and wrangling in another tool, SkyTree Adviser exposes machine-learning, statistics, and statistical graphics through an interface that is accessible to business analysts.

stack—which currently covers data processing, interactive (SQL) and streaming analysis.

What does *your* data science toolkit look like? Do you mainly use one stack or do you tend to mix and match?

Large-Scale Data Collection and Real-Time Analytics Using Redis

Insights from a Strata Santa Clara 2013 Session

By C. Aaron Cois (*http://oreil.ly/1al5MVE*)

Strata Santa Clara 2013 is a wrap, and I had a great time speaking and interacting with all of the amazing attendees. I'd like to recap the talk that Tim Palko (*http://bit.ly/1dpv3bx*) and I gave, entitled "Large-Scale Data Collection and Real-Time Analytics Using Redis," (*http://oreil.ly/1al5Nsq*) and maybe even answer a few questions we were asked following our time on stage.

Our talk centered around a system we designed to collect environmental sensor data from remote sensors located in various places across the country and provide real-time visualization, monitoring, and event detection. Our primary challenge for the initial phase of development proved to be scaling the system to collect data from thousands of nodes, each of which sent sensor readings roughly once per second, while maintaining the ability to query the data in real time for event detection. While each data record was only ~300 KBs, our expected maximum sensor load indicated a collection rate of about 27 million records, or 8 GBs, per hour. However, our primary issue was not data size, but data rate. A large number of inserts had to happen each second, and we were unable to buffer inserts into batches or transactions without incurring a delay in the real-time data stream.

When designing network applications, one must consider the two canonical I/O bottlenecks: network I/O, and filesystem I/O. For our use case, we had little influence over network I/O speeds. We had no control over the locations where our remote sensors would be deployed, or the bandwidth or network infrastructure of said facilities. With network latency as a known variant, we focused on addressing the bottleneck we could control: filesystem I/O. For the immediate collection problem, this means we evaluated databases to insert the data into as it was collected. While we initially attempted to collect the data in a relational database (PostgreSQL), we soon discovered that while PostgreSQL could potentially handle the number of inserts per second, it was unable to respond to read queries simultaneously. Simply put, we were unable to read data while we were collecting it, preventing us from doing any real-time analysis (or any analysis at all, for that matter, unless we stopped data collection).

The easiest way to avoid slowdowns due to filesystem operations is to avoid the filesystem altogether, a feat we achieved by leveraging Redis (*http://bit.ly/1dpv4MD*), an open source in-memory NoSQL data store. Redis stores all data in RAM, allowing lightning fast reads and writes. With Redis, we were easily able to insert all of our collected data as it was transmitted from the sensor nodes, and query the data simultaneously for event detection and analytics. In fact, we were also able to leverage Pub/Sub functionality on the same Redis server to publish notifications of detected events for transmission to SMTP workers, without any performance issues.

In addition to speed, Redis features advanced data structures, including lists, sets, hashes, and sorted sets, rather than the somewhat limiting key/value pair consistent with many NoSQL stores. Sorted sets proved to be an excellent data structure to model timeseries data, by setting the score to the timestamp of a given datapoint. This automatically ordered our timeseries, even when data was inserted out of order, and allowed querying by timestamp, timestamp range, or by "most recent number" of records (which is merely the last number values of the set).

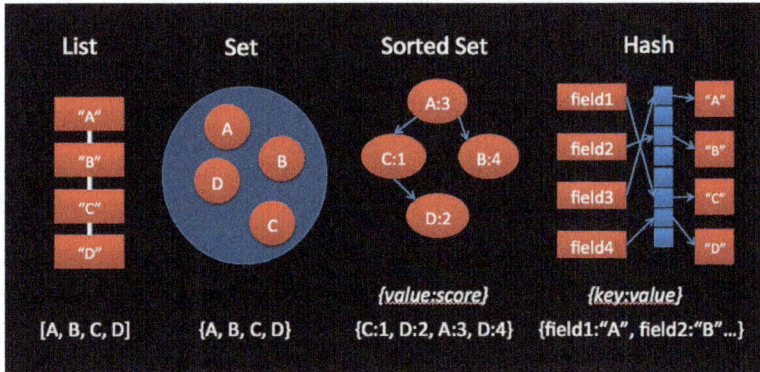

Of course, nothing is perfect, and our solution was no exception. Our use case requires us to archive our data permanently, for post analysis, rather than throwing away stale datapoints as is common in other real-time applications. Since Redis keeps all data in RAM, our Redis data store was only able to hold as much data as the server had RAM. Our data, inserted at a rate of 8 GB/hour, quickly outgrew this limitation. To scale this solution and archive our data for future analysis, we set up an automated migration script to push the oldest data in our Redis data store to a PostgreSQL database with more storage scalability. Writing a REST API as an interface to our two data stores allowed client applications a unified query interface, without having to worry about which data store a particular piece of data resided in.

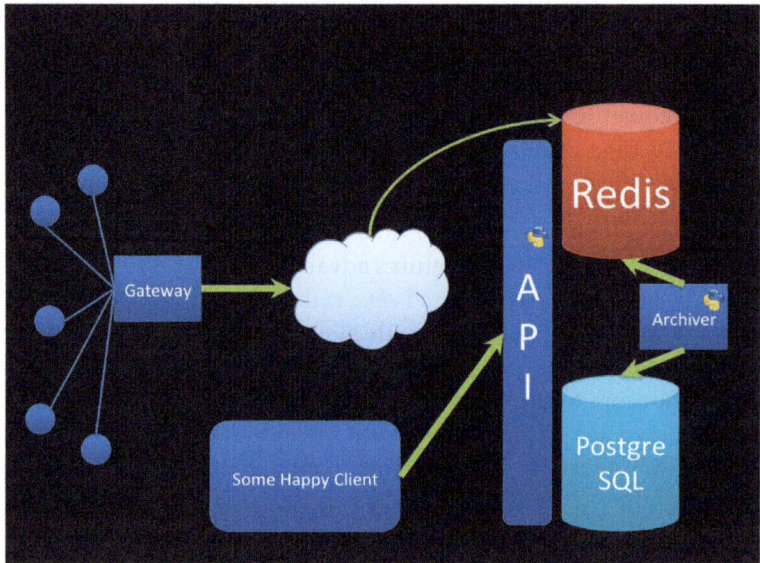

With the collection architecture described in place, generating automated event detection and real-time notifications was made easy, again through the use of Redis. Since Redis also offers Pub/Sub functionality, we were able to monitor incoming data in Redis using a small service, and push noteworthy events to a notification channel on the same Redis server, from which subscribed SMTP workers could send out notifications in real time.

Our experiences show Redis to be a powerful tool for big data applications, specifically for high-throughput data collection. The benefits of Redis as a collection mechanism, coupled with data migration to a deep analytics platform, such as relational databases or even Hadoop's HDFS, yields a powerful and versatile architecture suitable for many big data applications.

Returning Transactions to Distributed Data Stores

Principles for the next generation of NoSQL databases

By David Rosenthal (*http://linkd.in/1al5Lku*) and Stephen Pimentel (*http://linkd.in/1dpv3Z0*)

Database technologies are undergoing rapid evolution, with new approaches being actively explored after decades of relative stability. As late as 2008, the term "NoSQL" barely existed (*http://bit.ly/1al5NZC*) and relational databases were both commercially dominant and entrenched in the developer community. Since then, NoSQL systems have rapidly gained prominence and early systems such as Google's BigTable (*http://bit.ly/1dpv5A3*) and Amazon's Dynamo (*http://bit.ly/1al5OwJ*) have inspired dozens of new databases (HBase, Cassandra, Voldemort, MongoDB, etc.) that fall under the NoSQL umbrella.

The first generation of NoSQL databases aimed to achieve the dual goals of fault tolerance and horizontal scalability on clusters of commodity hardware. There are now a variety of NoSQL systems available that, at their best, achieve these goals. Unfortunately, the cost for these benefits is high: limited data model flexibility and extensibility, and weak guarantees for applications due to the lack of multistatement (global) transactions.

The Shadow of the CAP Theorem

This first generation of NoSQL databases was designed in the shadow of Brewer's CAP Theorem (*http://bit.ly/1dpv7rE*). In 2000, Eric Brewer conjectured (and Gilbert and Lynch (*http://bit.ly/1al5RII*) later proved) that a distributed system could simultaneously provide at most two out of three advantageous properties:

Consistency
　A read sees all previously completed writes.

Availability
　Reads and writes are always possible.

Partition tolerance
　Guaranteed properties are maintained even when network failures prevent some machines from communicating with others.

The theorem suggests three design options: **CP**, **AP**, and **CA**. In practice, for a decade after its formulation, CAP was interpreted as advocating **AP** systems (that is, sacrificing Consistency.) For example, in a paper explaining the design decisions made for the Dynamo database, Werner Vogels, the CTO of Amazon.com, wrote that "data inconsistency in large-scale reliable distributed systems has to be tolerated" (*http://bit.ly/1dpv6nC*) to obtain sufficient performance and availability.

Indeed, many NoSQL systems adopted similar logic and, in place of strong consistency, adopted a much weaker model called eventual consistency (*http://bit.ly/1al5Pkb*). Eventual consistency was considered a necessary evil, justified as an engineering trade-off necessary to deliver the other major goals of NoSQL. Even NoSQL systems that chose to stick with stronger consistency (e.g., HBase) decided to sacrifice *ACID transactions*—a powerful capability that has been available in the relational database management system (RDBMS) world for decades. It is this missing capability that limits each database to supporting a single, limited data model.

NoSQL Data Modeling

Each NoSQL database implements its own simple data model, such as a graph, document, column-family, or key/value store. Of course, different data models work better for different use cases, different languages, different applications, etc. All are simple enough that real-world applications will want to build up richer relations, indexes, or pointers within the simple structure of the base data model. Many application developers would even like to use different data models for different types of data. Unfortunately, application developers have no good way to use a NoSQL system to support multiple data models, or to build the abstractions needed to extend the base data model.

The key capability that the first generation of NoSQL systems lacks is *global ACID transactions*. Though many NoSQL systems claim support of ACID transactions, they are almost never referring to *global ACID* transactions that allow multiple arbitrary operations in a single transaction. The local ACID transactions that they provide are better than nothing, but are fundamentally unable to enforce rules, relationships, or constraints between multiple pieces of data—the key to enabling strong abstractions.

Revisiting the CAP Theorem

Experience with these challenges has led some of the original thought leaders of the NoSQL movement to reexamine the CAP theorem and reassess the space of realistic engineering possibilities. In 2010, Vogels wrote that it is indeed possible to provide strong consistency and that Amazon would add such consistency as an option in their SimpleDB product. He warned that "achieving strict consistency can come at a cost in update or read latency, and may result in lower throughput." Rather than claiming that data inconsistency simply "has to be tolerated," he now advised that benefits of strong consistency must be balanced against performance costs. He did not, however, attempt to characterize the magnitude of these costs.

In 2012, Brewer wrote that the CAP theorem has been widely misunderstood (*http://bit.ly/1dpv6E7*). In particular, he noted that "the '2 of 3' formulation was always misleading" and that "CAP prohibits only a tiny part of the design space: perfect availability and consistency in the presence of partitions, which are rare." This point is fundamental because the CAP notion of availability actually refers to a property called *perfect availability*: that reads and writes are always possible *from every machine, even if it is partitioned from the network*.

This property is very different from the *availability* of the database as a whole to a client. Reconsideration of the design space leads to the surprising conclusion that sacrificing CAP theorem availability does not exclude building a highly available database. By keeping multiple replicas of database state on multiple machines, a consistent database can stay available to clients even when some replicas are down. Even better, with consistency maintained, the possibility of supporting global transactions emerges.

Return to ACID

As developers have gained experience working with **AP** systems and with **CP** systems without transactions, they have come to understand the heavy engineering cost of working around these weaker guarantees. This cost is leading some distributed database designers to reconsider **CP** systems with global transactions.

Google exemplifies this trend with their new Spanner (*http://bit.ly/T9LHpZ*) database, a **CP** database with global transactions intended to replace their first-generation NoSQL database, BigTable, across a wide range of applications. Spanner is Google's first major distributed database not built on top of BigTable and supports the same multidatacenter operation.

Internally, Google "consistently received complaints from users that BigTable can be difficult to use." In particular, "the lack of cross-row [global] transactions in BigTable led to frequent complaints." As a result, the designers of Spanner now believe that "it is better to have application programmers deal with performance problems due to overuse of transactions as bottlenecks arise, rather than always coding around the lack of transactions."

Spanner has been widely noted in the NoSQL field because it serves as an "existence proof" that distributed databases providing global transactions at scale are feasible. Spanner further demonstrates that a distributed database can remain highly available (*http://bit.ly/1dpv9Qf*) over a broad range of failures without supporting availability in the CAP sense.

FoundationDB

FoundationDB (*http://bit.ly/1al5SMT*) is a NoSQL database that uses a distributed design and presents a single logical ordered-key-value data model. Unlike many other NoSQL databases, FoundationDB presents a single consistent state and supports global transactions.

Like all **CP** systems, FoundationDB chooses **C** over **A** during network partitions; when multiple machines or data centers are unable to communicate, some of them will be unable to execute writes. Nevertheless, in a wide variety of real-world failure modes, the database and the application using it will remain up. Leader election algorithms and data replication avoid a single point of failure. To achieve this during a partition, FoundationDB needs to determine which side of the partition should continue to accept reads and writes. To avoid a *split brain* scenario (where each side of a network partition thinks it is the authority), FoundationDB uses an odd-numbered group of *coordination servers*. Using the Paxos algorithm, FoundationDB determines which partition contains a majority of these coordination servers and only allows that partition to remain responsive to writes.

Of course, the logic to handle consistency and global transactions does create some overhead that, as Vogels noted in his 2010 post, imposes costs in latencies and throughput. FoundationDB has sought to both measure and reduce these costs. During a benchmark (*http://bit.ly/*

1dpva6S) on a 24-node cluster with a workload of cross-node multi-statement global transactions, FoundationDB uses less than 10% of total CPU capacity to support those guarantees.

A New Generation of NoSQL

Systems such as Spanner and FoundationDB suggest an approach for a new generation of NoSQL. Like the first generation, the new systems will employ shared-nothing, distributed architectures with fault tolerance and scalability. However, rather than default to designs with weak consistency, the new generation will aggressively explore the strong-consistency region of the design space actually permitted by the CAP theorem, and with it the possibility of true global transactions.

Though there is a strong correlation between global transactions and a relational data model in currently implemented systems, there is no deep reason for that correlation and every reason to bring global transactions to NoSQL as well. The power of this combination is that it supports abstractions and extensions to the basic NoSQL data models that make building applications much easier. To achieve this design potential, the new generation should follow three broad principles:

1. Maintain what works about NoSQL, especially those things that make NoSQL great: distributed design, fault tolerance, easy scaling, and a simple, flexible base data model. A storage system that offers these properties and can handle both random access and streaming workloads efficiently could support a huge range of types of data and applications.

2. Leverage our modern understanding of CAP to support global transactions: global transactions can be implemented in a distributed, scalable manner as demonstrated by Spanner and FoundationDB. The benefits to applications and application developers are dramatic and greatly outweigh the theoretical performance penalty.

3. Build richer data models as abstractions: extend the base data models of NoSQL and build richer data models using the strength of global transactions. This approach allows a single database to support multiple data models, enabling applications to select the models best suited to their problem. This will provide true data model flexibility within a single database system.

By following the above principles, the next generation of NoSQL databases will provide a solid foundation that supports a vibrant ecosystem of data models, frameworks, and applications.

Data Science Tools: Fast, Easy to Use, and Scalable

Tools slowly democratize many data science tasks

By Ben Lorica (*http://bit.ly/1dptMRz*)

Here are a few observations based on conversations I had during the just concluded Strata Santa Clara conference.

Spark Is Attracting Attention

I've written numerous times about components of the Berkeley Data Analytics Stack (Spark, Shark, MLbase). Two Spark-related sessions at Strata were packed (slides here (*http://oreil.ly/1dpvcf0*) and here (*http://oreil.ly/1al5Tk0*)) and I talked to many people who were itching to try the BDAS stack (*http://bit.ly/1al4Xfo*). Being able to combine batch, real-time, and interactive analytics in a framework that uses a simple programming model is very attractive. The release of version 0.7 (*http://bit.ly/1al5TQY*) adds a Python API to Spark's native Scala interface and Java API.

SQL Is Alive and Well

Impala's well-received launch at Strata NYC last fall confirmed the strong interest in *interactive analytics* (ad hoc query and response) within the Hadoop ecosystem. The list of solutions (*http://bit.ly/1dpvd2t*) for querying big data (stored in HDFS) continues to grow with CitusDB and Pivotal HD, joining Impala, Shark, Hadapt, and cloud-based alternatives BigQuery, Redshift, and Qubole. I use Shark and have been impressed by its speed and ease of use. (I've heard similar things about Impala's speed recently.)

Business Intelligence Reboot (Again)

QlikTech and Tableau (*http://bit.ly/1al5QVj*) had combined 2012 revenues of more than $450 million. They are easy-to-use analysis tools that let users visually explore data, as well as share charts and dashboards. Both use in-memory technologies to speed up query response and visualization rendering times. Both run only on MS Windows.

Startups that draw inspiration from these two successful companies are targeting much larger data sets—in the case of Datameer and Platfora, and Karmasphere, massive data sets stored in HDFS. Platfora has been generating buzz with its fast in-memory, columnar data store, custom HTML5 visualization package, and emphasis on tools that let users interact with massive data. Datameer continues to quietly rack up sales—it closed 2012 with more than $10 million in revenues (*http://bit.ly/1al5QVj*). Strata Startup Showcase (audience choice) winner SiSense offers a hardware optimized business analytics platform that delivers fast processing times by efficiently utilizing disk, RAM, and CPU.

Scalable Machine Learning and Analytics Are Going to Get Simpler

In previous posts I detailed why I like GraphChi/ GraphLab (*http://bit.ly/1dpuUVo*) and why I'm excited about MLbase (*http://bit.ly/1al4v0N*). Two other open source projects are worth highlighting: Mahout has many more algorithms (*http:// bit.ly/1al5Vbr*) but VW (*http://bit.ly/1dpvdQe*) generates more enthusiastic endorsements from users I've spoken with. However the sparse documentation and the many command-line options makes it tough to get going in VW. (A forthcoming O'Reilly book should make VW more accessible.) For users who want to roll their own, I've written a few simple distributed, machine-learning algorithms in Spark, and found it quite fast for batch training and scoring.

H20 is a new, open source, machine-learning platform from 0xdata. It can use data stored in HDFS or flat files and comes with a few *distributed* algorithms (random forests, GLM, and a few others). H20 also has tools for rudimentary exploratory data analysis and wrangling. Users can navigate the system using a web browser or a command-line interface. Just like Revolution Analytics' ScaleR, users can interact with H20 using R code (limited to the subset of models and algorithms available). H20 is also available via REST/JSON interfaces.

What I found intriguing was SkyTree's acquisition of AdviseAnalytics —a desktop software product designed to make statistical data analysis accessible. (AdviseAnalytics was founded by Leland Wilkinson (http://bit.ly/1al5VrV), creator of the popular Systat software package and author of *The Grammar of Graphics* (http://amzn.to/19lKFe3).) The system now called SkyTree Adviser provides a GUI that emphasizes *tasks* (cluster, classify, compare, etc.) over algorithms. In addition, it produces results that include short explanations of the underlying statistical methods (power users can opt for concise results similar to those produced by standard statistical packages). Finally, SkyTree Adviser users benefit from the vast number of algorithms available—the system uses ensembles, or finds optimal algorithms. (The MLbase optimizer (http://bit.ly/1al4v0N) will perform the same type of automatic "model selection" for *distributed* algorithms.)

SkyTree now offers users an easy-to-use tool for analytic explorations over medium-sized data sets (SkyTree Adviser), and a server product (http://bit.ly/1dpvfrf) for building and deploying algorithms against massive amounts of data. Throw in MLbase and Hazy (http://bit.ly/1al5VZ5), and I can see the emergence of several large-scale machine-learning tools[61] for nontechnical users.

Reproducibility of Data Science Workflows

COMPUTER SCIENCE	MATHEMATICS, STATISTICS, AND DATA MINING	GRAPHIC DESIGN	INFOVIS AND HCI
acquire parse	filter mine	represent refine	interact

Source: "Computational Information Design" by Ben Fry

Data scientists tend to use many tools, and the frequent context switching is a drag on their productivity. An important side effect is that it's often challenging to document and reproduce analysis projects that involve many steps and tools.

Data scientists who rely on the Python data stack (Numpy (http://bit.ly/1al5Wfv), SciPy (http://bit.ly/1dpvhPQ), Pandas (http://bit.ly/1al5Zbd), nltk, etc.) should check out Wakari from Continuum Analytics. It's a cloud-based service that takes care of many details, in-

---

61. BI tools like Datameer already come with simple analytic functions (http://bit.ly/1al5IVL) available through a GUI.

cluding data, package, and version management, while insulating the user from the intricacies of Amazon Web Services.

Loom (*http://bit.ly/1al5H45*) is a just-released data management system that initially targets users of Hadoop (and R). By letting users track lineage and data provenance (*http://oreil.ly/1al5ZrS*), Loom makes it easier to re-create multistep data analysis projects.

MATLAB, R, and Julia: Languages for Data Analysis

Inside core features of specialized data analysis languages

By Avi Bryant (*http://oreil.ly/1dpvgLJ*)

Big data frameworks like Hadoop have received a lot of attention recently, and with good reason: when you have terabytes of data to work with—and these days, who doesn't?—it's amazing to have affordable, reliable, and ubiquitous tools that allow you to spread a computation over tens or hundreds of CPUs on commodity hardware. The dirty truth is, though, that many analysts and scientists spend as much time or more working with mere megabytes or gigabytes of data: a small sample pulled from a larger set, or the aggregated results of a Hadoop job, or just a data set that isn't all that big (like, say, all of Wikipedia, which can be squeezed into a few gigs without too much trouble).

At this scale, you don't need a fancy distributed framework. You can just load the data into memory and explore it interactively in your favorite scripting language. Or, maybe, a different scripting language: data analysis is one of the few domains where special-purpose languages are very commonly used. Although in many respects these are similar to other dynamic languages like Ruby or Javascript, these languages have syntax and built-in data structures that make common data analysis tasks both faster and more concise. This article will briefly cover some of these core features for two languages that have been popular for decades—MATLAB and R—and another, Julia, that was just announced this year.

MATLAB

MATLAB (*http://bit.ly/1al61Qp*) is one of the oldest programming languages designed specifically for data analysis, and it is still extremely popular today. MATLAB was conceived in the late '70s as a simple scripting language wrapped around the FORTRAN libraries LINPACK and EISPACK, which at the time were the best way to efficiently work with large matrices of data—as they arguably still are, through their successor LAPACK (*http://bit.ly/1dpviTS*). These libraries, and thus MATLAB, were solely concerned with one data type: the matrix, a two-dimensional array of numbers.

This may seem very limiting, but in fact, a very wide range of scientific and data-analysis problems can be represented as matrix problems, and often very efficiently. Image processing, for example, is an obvious fit for the 2-D data structure; less obvious, perhaps, is that a directed graph (like Twitter's Follow graph, or the graph of all links on the Web) can be expressed as an adjacency matrix (*http://bit.ly/1al60fj*), and that graph algorithms like Google's PageRank (*http://bit.ly/1dpvjaq*) can be easily implemented as a series of additions and multiplications of these matrices. Similarly, the winning entry (*http://soc.att.com/1al60vM*) to the Netflix Prize recommendation challenge relied, in part, on a matrix representation of everyone's movie ratings (you can imagine every row representing a Netflix user, every column a movie, and every entry in the matrix a rating), and in particular on an operation called Singular Value Decomposition (*http://bit.ly/19lC3UC*), one of those original LINPACK matrix routines that MATLAB was designed to make easy to use.

Its focus on matrices led to some important differences in MATLAB's design compared to general-purpose programming languages. First, it has special syntax for matrix literals. For simple cases, this will look pretty familiar; here's a 1×2 matrix (in other words, a row vector):

```
V = [1 2]
```

Here's a 2×3 matrix (the semicolon is what breaks up the rows; the line break is ignored):

```
A = [4 5 6;
     7 8 9]
```

It gets more interesting when you take advantage of interpolation. As with strings in some other languages, in MATLAB you can mix matrix variables in with literal data, almost like a template. For example, given the above definitions, then this:

```
B = [V 3; A]
```

will produce this 3×3 matrix:

```
B =

     1     2     3
     4     5     6
     7     8     9
```

In two dimensions, it's a little trickier to fit things together than with strings. If we hadn't included the "3" to pad out the first row, the interpreter would have complained that the dimensions don't match, and the literal would have been invalid.

More important than the literal syntax is that all of the core library functions and operators in MATLAB were designed to accept and return matrices rather than individual values. This can take some getting used to. It may not seem that strange that we can double every element of our matrix above by adding it to itself:

```
BB = B + B

BB =

     2     4     6
     8    10    12
    14    16    18
```

Or even that a function like sqrt will take the square root of every element:

```
BR = sqrt(B)

BR =

    1.0000    1.4142    1.7321
    2.0000    2.2361    2.4495
    2.6458    2.8284    3.0000
```

It's a little bit more strange to pass it to a function like isprime and get a matrix back as a result, with a "1" in every matrix location that held a prime number:

```
BP = isprime(B)

BP =

     0     1     1
     0     1     0
     1     0     0
```

It's also strangely powerful to be able to naturally extend algorithms into multiple dimensions. For example, in most programming languages, if we had a column of numbers and wanted to find the mean, it would be straightforward to sum up the column and divide by the number of rows:

```
C = [1; 2; 3; 4; 5; 6; 7]
mean = sum(C) / rows(C)

mean = 4
```

But let's say that instead we had a matrix where each row represented an (x,y) point:

```
D = [3 4;
     2 0;
     6 1;
     1 3]
```

Plotted, it looks like this:

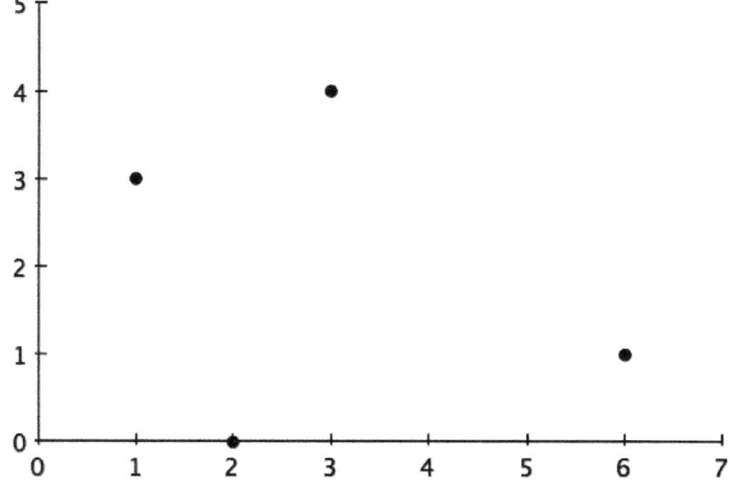

Because sum( ) works on columns, no matter how many there are, we can use the exact same code to find the center—technically, the centroid (*http://bit.ly/1a1mbcW*)—of these points, which has the mean of all the x values for its x, and the mean of all the y values for its y:

```
center = sum(D) / rows(D)

center =

    3    2
```

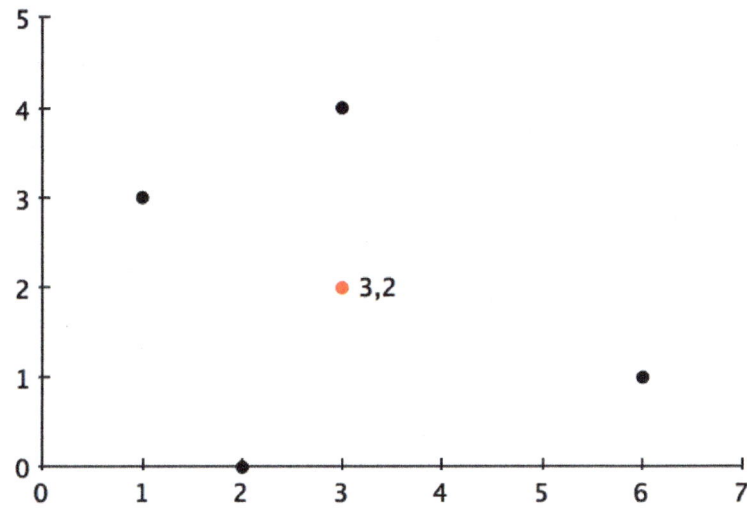

What if we wanted to find the distance from each point to that center? Again, we can operate on the matrix as a whole. Distance is the square root of the sum of the squares of the differences for each dimension, or in MATLAB:

```
distances = sqrt(sum(power(D - center, 2), 2))

distances =

   2.0000
   2.2361
   3.1623
   2.2361
```

(If you're wondering why we're passing a 2 to sum(), that's because we're asking to sum the rows—the second dimension—rather than columns, which is the default.)

All of this would also work unchanged for points with three (or more!) dimensions, simply by adding more columns to our original matrix.

The other important feature to call out in MATLAB's matrix syntax is the very flexible support for indexing into a matrix. You can, of course, pick out an individual element—for example, D(1,1) picks out row 1, column 1 of D—but you can also use ranges, or wildcards. For example, because a colon by itself acts as a wildcard, Dy = D(:,2) will pick out the second (y) column for each row in D:

```
Dy =

    4
    0
    1
    3
```

You can also use "logical indexing" to index a matrix by another matrix: M(I) will return only those elements in M that correspond to nonzero elements of I. To return to our earlier example, `primes = B(BP)` would return only those elements of B that are prime, and thus have corresponding 1s in the BP matrix:

```
primes =

    7
    2
    5
    3
```

Because logical and comparison operators also work on matrices, you can use this almost like a little query language. For example, this will return all elements of B that are both prime and greater than 5:

```
result = B(isprime(B) & (B > 5))

result = 7
```

Just to reiterate what's happening here: each of `isprime(B)` and `B > 5` are returning matrices full of 0s and 1s; the & operator is combining them; the resulting matrix is being used to index into B and return the (single, in this case) result of 7. And yet, it reads almost like SQL.

It's worth mentioning that MATLAB is commercial software; throughout these examples, I've in fact been using GNU Octave (*http://bit.ly/1dpvkLu*), an open source language designed to be compatible in most respects.

R

The other widely used open source language for data analysis is R, a modern version of the S language for statistical computing that originally came out of the Bell Labs around the same time MATLAB was being developed.

Although R has access to a similar set of matrix math routines as MATLAB—via the LAPACK library—it avoids any specialized syntax for numeric matrices. Where R shines, instead, is in data sets that are richer or messier than the pure numerics of MATLAB. R introduces the "data frame" as a core data structure, which is like a matrix with two key differences: first, its columns and rows can have names; second, each column can hold a different data type. Like MATLAB matrices, you can operate on them as a whole. For example, our centroid example from earlier would look like this in R:

```
D = data.frame(x = c(3,2,6,1), y=c(4,0,1,3))
center = colSums(D) / nrow(D)

center =
  x y
  3 2
```

Even in this simple example, and even without making use of multiple data types in the columns, it's awfully convenient to see named columns rather than just numeric indices. R exploits the names for much more than just output, however. First, it has specialized syntax for referencing a column by name. Although we could index the second column with D[,2] (unlike MATLAB, instead of using a specific wildcard character, we just omit the row index that would go before the comma), we can also reference it more simply:

```
D$y

[1] 4 0 1 3
```

Even more simply, in the common case where we are working primarily with one data set, we can use R's `attach()` function to import the column names into our local variable scope. (Experienced R users would, however, warn you against using this in more complex cases where you had multiple data sets, or a large number of columns, since you can quickly and confusingly clutter up your scope). Once we've attached D, we can access its columns just as x and y. If we wanted to compute, say, a new column that was the product of D's x and y columns, nothing could be easier:

```
attach(D)
x * y

[1] 12 0 6 3
```

Unlike matrices, R's data frames can also be extended with new rows or columns, so that we could create a new column for this result if we liked:

```
D$xy = x * y
```

However, because this column didn't exist when we performed the attach(), it won't be available as a local variable unless we attach(D) again.

R can do the same logical indexing tricks that MATLAB can, but they work even better with attached named columns. Let's say we had a data frame with columns for height, weight, and gender:

```
M = data.frame(height = c(62, 70, 67), weight = c(120, 178, 180),
gender = c("m", "f", "m"))
attach(M)
```

We can use logical operations on the column variables to produce a vector of Booleans, showing us which rows represent men taller than 65":

```
height > 65 & gender == "m"
```

```
[1] FALSE FALSE  TRUE
```

But as with MATLAB, we can also use that vector to index into the rows of the original data frame, returning (in this case) the single matching result:

```
M[height > 65 & gender == "m",]

   height weight gender
       67    180      m
```

Note the comma at the end, which ensures that this is interpreted as a row index and that we get all columns. (For this specific case, it would also be idiomatic to use the subset() function, which operates similarly but doesn't require attach().)

Finally, attaching named columns also makes it easy to use another piece of special-purpose R syntax: model formula notation. This allows you to express a relationship between two or more variables and is used pervasively throughout R. Functions for plotting, regression and ANOVA, machine learning, and so on can all make use of models described in this form. For example, if we believed there was a linear relationship between the height values and the weight values of D, we might ask R to try to fit this model like so, using the lm() linear model function:

```
model = lm(weight ~ height)
```

Similarly, we could bring up a scatter plot with just:

```
plot(weight ~ height)
```

If we believed that weight depended on both height and gender, we could express that as weight ~ height + gender. More complicated relationships are possible, too, within limits; for example, the * operator can be used to relate two variables that interact rather than being independent. It would be unusual for a general-purpose language to have built-in syntax for defining these kinds of models; because R was designed for statistics, it's both available and widely used, and helps greatly in allowing complex, highly configurable features like plotting or generalized linear modeling to be hidden behind a single function call.

MATLAB and R both share this style of exposing very complex functionality through a single function, often with a huge number of optional parameters. For example, R's plot function literally can take dozens of graphical parameters, and MATLAB's isn't far behind. Functions for optimization, clustering, regression, and so on are similar, if less extreme. This works very well for the common case of loading a research data set into an interactive session and exploring it using the standard library toolkit—especially when you have something like model formula notation to keep the default usage very simple. It can be daunting, however, to dive deeper and build larger programs that need to extend, tweak, or reuse parts of this toolkit because a function like plot() or lm() appears to be a black box; either you need exactly what it does, or you need to reimplement the whole thing.

This is certainly not universally true; most would probably agree that Hadley Wickham's plyr (*http://bit.ly/1al63b4*) and ggplot2 (*http://bit.ly/1dpvmTF*) packages, for example, have elegantly composable APIs. But the underlying structures of these languages may not encourage this kind of careful design. It's telling, for example, that MATLAB awkwardly requires a separate file for each and every public function, or that John Myles White's excellent R-focused blog describes (*http://bit.ly/1al63rB*) object-oriented programming in R as "a hack that was put on top of the original S language," and has trouble puzzling out what the right style is for defining setter methods. It's also telling that while a tutorial for a general-purpose language like Python will cover defining functions and classes early on, many R and MATLAB tutorials never cover these topics at all.

Performance may also be a factor. Although they can do matrix math very fast, thanks to the underlying libraries, both MATLAB and R have notoriously slow language interpreters (and this goes double for the open source Octave implementation). This discourages writing large libraries or complex abstractions in the languages themselves and tends to relegate the computational core of any new function to a C or FORTRAN extension, which makes the function even more of a daunting black box to the casual hacker.

Julia

Julia (*http://bit.ly/1al4IRr*) is a modern language for scientific computing, designed to address some of these concerns. Superficially, Julia strongly resembles MATLAB. For example, here's how the MATLAB documentation says you should compute the density of a matrix—that is, what proportion of its values are nonzero:

```
x = [1 0 3 0; 4 3 0 1; 2 3 5 5]
density = nnz(x)/prod(size(x))

density = 0.75
```

To unpack this a little bit: the obscurely named nnz function returns the number of nonzero values in the matrix; size() returns a vector with the matrix dimensions (in this case, [3 4]); and prod() multiplies up all the values in that vector, giving us the total number of entries in the matrix. Simple division gives us the density.

Here's the equivalent code in Julia:

```
x = [1 0 3 0; 4 3 0 1; 2 3 5 5]
density = nnz(x)/prod(size(x))
```

Well, not just equivalent, but identical! Matrix literals and obscure function names and all. Most code won't port over quite this easily, but Julia is clearly designed to make MATLAB users feel at home. Under the hood, however, things look extremely different. It's instructive to look at Julia's implementation of the prod function and compare it to Octave's (since we don't have access to MATLAB's). Here's a snippet of Octave's prod:

```
DEFUN (prod, args, ,
  "prod (X): products")
{
  octave_value_list retval;

  int nargin = args.length ();
  if (nargin == 1) {
      octave_value arg = args(0);
```

```
        if (arg.is_real_type ()) {
          Matrix tmp = arg.matrix_value ();
          if (! error_state)
                retval(0) = tmp.prod ();
        } else if (arg.is_complex_type ()) {
          …
        } else {
            gripe_wrong_type_arg ("prod", arg);
            return retval;
          }
      } else {
          …
      }
}
```

A few things to notice: first of all, Octave implements this and many of the standard library functions in C; second, there are hardcoded checks for the number of arguments, and for two possible argument types—a standard real-valued matrix and a complex matrix—with calls to separate implementations for each, where the actual computation happens.

Here's the equivalent code in Julia:

```
function prod{T}(A::StridedArray{T})
    if isempty(A)
        return one(T)
    end
    v = A[1]
    for i=2:numel(A)
        v *= A[i]
    end
    v
end
```

It's considerably shorter and easier to read, mostly because—even though it's a core function—it's implemented in Julia itself. It's also generic, which is to say, this one piece of code will work for integer matrices, or complex, or double-precision, and so on. StridedArray is Julia's type for dense (as opposed to sparse) type parameter and can take on any value, including a user-supplied type. An especially interesting thing here is the behavior when the array is empty: even though it doesn't have any example values to work with, it can pass the type parameter to the one() function to get a "1" of the right type.

It's also important to point out that even though these arrays are generic, they're not boxed: an Int8 array will take up much less memory than an Int64 array, and both will be laid out as continuous blocks of memory; Julia can deal seamlessly and generically with these different immediate types as well as pointer types like String.

In MATLAB, if you define a new data type, it's possible to provide alternative implementations of functions like prod that operate on that type. The same is true of Julia: the implementation shown above is only used for StridedArray, and Julia provides entirely separate implementations for other types—like DArray, Julia's distributed array implementation.

Unlike in MATLAB, Julia also lets you provide alternative implementations for more subtle variations. For example, the specific case of a dense array of Booleans is overridden to error:

```
prod(A::StridedArray{Bool})  =  error("use  all()  instead  of prod()  for boolean arrays")
```

Julia has full multiple dispatch, meaning that the implementation is chosen based on the specific type (and number) of all of the arguments to the function—which is why the Octave code above has an explicit check for the number of arguments but Julia doesn't. Here's a variation that allows you to pass an extra argument specifying which dimension to multiply on (like the extra 2 passed to sum() in the MATLAB example computing distances):

```
prod{T}(A::StridedArray{T}, region::Dimspec) = areduce(*,A,region,one(T))
```

This is extremely concise because it's implemented with higher-order functions, passing the * function as a value to a generic array reduction function—if you passed in + instead, you'd have sum(). Julia makes extensive use of this functional programming style, allowing its core library to be implemented at a high level of abstraction. Abstraction can be costly, but it's made possible in Julia by a very high-performance language implementation.

How high performance? The Julia site lists a handful of benchmarks comparing R, MATLAB, and Julia (as well as some others). For tasks that mostly exercise the underlying matrix libraries, like random matrix multiplication, they all do similarly well, as does C. For tasks that exercise basic language features, like a simple recursive fibonacci implementation, Julia is a few times slower than C but is around 100 times faster than R and nearly 1,000 times faster than MATLAB or Octave. This is a stunning difference, and may sound too good to be true, but although microbenchmarks should certainly be taken with a grain of salt, and these come from an obviously biased source, there's no reason to think that Julia can't be that fast. As an existence proof, Google's V8 JavaScript engine gets very similar performance from a language that's even more dynamic and difficult to optimize; matching it is impressive but certainly not impossible. (Google has Lars Bak, a master virtual machine implementer with decades of experience starting with the influential SELF project, but the Julia team, like anyone else, has access to those same influential papers).

Julia's weakness, however, is its libraries. R has CRAN (*http://bit.ly/1al63HV*), certainly the most impressive collection of statistical libraries available anywhere. MATLAB also has a wide range of toolboxes (*http://bit.ly/1dpvnqI*) available, for a price. Julia also lacks a rich development environment, like RStudio (*http://bit.ly/1al63I6*), and has only rudimentary support for plotting, which is a pretty critical part of most exploratory data analysis. Julia does, however, have a very active community, and I hope and believe that the rest will come with time; for now, it's hard to compete with the decades of accumulated contributions that the older languages have.

...and Python

Reading this, you might get the impression that data analysis is all about numerics and filtering, and maybe plotting. Of course, that's not true in the real world: data is messy, and in many cases, the majority of the work in a data analysis project is retrieving the data, parsing it, munging it, and so on. In this area, it's unfortunately hard to dispute that general-purpose scripting languages like Perl, Ruby, and Python have much better language and library support in this area than any of the data-specific languages. For that reason, despite the obvious advantages of MATLAB, R, and Julia, it's also always worth considering what a general-purpose language can bring to the table.

The leading contender here is almost certainly Python. The NumPy (*http://bit.ly/1al63I6*) library provides a solid MATLAB-like matrix data structure, with efficient matrix and vector operations. That's not unusual, however. For example, NArray (*http://bit.ly/1al64eX*) provides a similar facility for Ruby; Java and the various JVM languages can use Colt (*http://1.usa.gov/1dpvoe6*), and so on. What makes Python stand out are two more libraries that have been built on top of NumPy:

- SciPy (*http://bit.ly/1al67aE*) includes a very large collection of numerical, statistical, and optimization algorithms.
- Wes McKinney's Pandas (*http://bit.ly/1al5Zbd*) provides R-style Data Frame objects (using NumPy arrays underneath to ensure fast computation), along with a wealth of tools for manipulating them.

At the same time, Python has a huge number of well-known libraries for the messier parts of analysis. For example, Beautiful Soup (*http://bit.ly/1a1mRit*) is best-of-breed for quickly scraping and parsing real-world HTML. Together with Python's strong community and innovative environments like iPython (*http://bit.ly/1a1kFr4*) and Reinteract (*http://bit.ly/1al65Qg*), these libraries make Python a compelling alternative: not as tuned to numerics as MATLAB, or to stats as R, or as fast or elegant as Julia, but a useful (and popular) tool for data analysis all the same.

Google's Spanner Is All About Time

Did Google just prove the industry wrong? Early thoughts on the Spanner database

By Tim O'Brien (*http://bit.ly/1dpvqmu*)

In case you missed it, Google Research published another one of "those" significant research papers (*http://bit.ly/T9LHpZ*)—a paper like the BigTable paper (*http://bit.ly/1dpvqTo*) from 2006 that had ramifications for the entire industry (that paper was one of the opening volleys in the NoSQL movement).

Google's new paper is about a distributed relational database called Spanner (*http://bit.ly/T9LHpZ*) that was a follow up to a presentation from earlier in the year about a new database for AdWords called F1 (*http://bit.ly/1dpvra0*). If you recall, that presentation revealed Google's migration of AdWords from MySQL to a new database that supported SQL and hierarchical schemas—two ideas that buck the trend from relational databases.

Meet Spanner

This new database, Spanner, is a database unlike anything we've seen. It's a database that embraces ACID, SQL, and transactions, that can be distributed across thousands of nodes spanning multiple data centers across multiple regions. The paper dwells on two main features that define this database:

Schematized Semi-Relational Tables
A hierarchical approach to grouping tables that allows Spanner to co-locate related data into directories that can be easily stored, replicated, locked, and managed on what Google calls spanservers. They have a modified SQL syntax that allows for the data to be interleaved, and the paper mentions some changes to support columns encoded with Protobufs.

Reification of Clock Uncertainty
This is the real emphasis of the paper. The missing link in relational database scalability was a strong emphasis on coordination backed by a serious attempt to minimize time uncertainty. In Google's new global-scale database, the variable that matters is epsilon—time uncertainty. Google has achieved very low overhead (*14 ms introduced by Spanner in this paper for data centers at 1 ms network distance*) for read-write (RW) transactions that span U.S. East Coast and U.S. West Coast (data centers separated by around 2 ms of network time) by creating a system that facilitates distributed transactions bound only by network distance (measured in milliseconds) and time uncertainty (epsilon).

Correction
Peter Norton (*http://bit.ly/1al66DH*) points out the obvious: 14 ms coast-to-coast (US) is impossible. Light over glass takes at least 40 ms to cross North America. Google ran these tests on networks at 1 ms network distance.

A Spanner deployment consists of a few management servers to manage multiple zones across data centers. A zone master and a series of location proxies manage hundreds or thousands of spanservers that perform the bulk of the work in the Spanner database. Spanservers house units of data called directories and each of these units implements a Paxos state machine atop something called a tablet. Spanservers store data in B-trees using a composite key alongside a timestamp and a value.

What's a Paxos state machine? From Wikipedia (*http://bit.ly/1dpvrGM*):

Paxos is a family of protocols for solving consensus (*http://bit.ly/ 1al69zf*) in a network of unreliable processors. **Consensus** is the process of agreeing on one result among a group of participants. This problem becomes difficult when the participants or their communication medium may experience failures.

In other words, Paxos is about figuring out consensus under potentially sketchy circumstances. This is very important to Spanner because each of these spanserver nodes needs to be able to elect itself a leader for a transaction; Paxos provides a mechanism to ensure consensus about which node is running a particular transaction.

Think of Spanner as a database whose data is distributed among thousands (tens of thousands) of these spanservers, each relying on zone masters and other servers to keep track of the location of data and direct them to spanservers using Paxos and other protocols to coordinate and manage read-write transactions among themselves. All of this is made possible because Spanner's TrueTime API allows each node participating in a transaction to minimize time uncertainty.

Clocks Galore: Armageddon Masters and GPS Clocks

To implement a continent-wide relational database with support for distributed two-phase commits that would complete in a reasonable amount of time (14.1 ms), Google had to find a way to master time. In Spanner, there are snapshot reads that don't need to read the latest timestamp, there are read transactions that need more of a guarantee that they are reading the latest version, and then there are read-write transactions. And read-write transactions that can span multiple spanservers in different datacenters is the real prize. Read the paper (*http://bit.ly/T9LHpZ*) and you can see what has to happen to a group of these spanservers to coordinate. Here's a segment that describes what happens in a read-write transaction:

> [The coordinator leader] first acquires write locks, but skips the prepare phase. It chooses a timestamp for the entire transaction after hearing from all other participant leaders. The commit timestamps must be greater or equal to all prepared timestamps ... and greater than any timestamps the leader has assigned to previous transactions (again, to preserve monotonicity). The coordinator leader then logs a commit record through Paxos (or an abort if it timed out while waiting on the other participants).

In essence, RW transactions are possible because low time uncertainty reduces the amount of time that these independent leaders in a transaction need to wait to conclude that consensus has been reached. There's a built-in latency of 2 * epsilon, and a good deal of the paper is focused on how Google now focuses on reducing time uncertainty. Time uncertainty has now become the metric to measure for Spanner.

"An Atomic Clock Is Not that Expensive"

When you read one of these seminal Google papers you always reach a moment that makes you pause in disbelief. Case in point, here's the paragraph from the Spanner paper that discusses the infrastructure (*http://bit.ly/T9LHpZ*) that supports a new Time API called TrueTime:

> TrueTime is implemented by a set of time master machines per data center and a timeslave daemon per machine. The majority of masters have GPS receivers with dedicated antennas; these masters are separated physically to reduce the effects of antenna failures, radio interference, and spoofing. The remaining masters (which we refer to as Armageddon masters) are equipped with atomic clocks. An atomic clock is not that expensive: the cost of an Armageddon master is of the same order as that of a GPS master.

The Evolution of Persistence at Google

In the beginning there was BigTable…BigTable was the inspiration for Cassandra, HBase, and a number of other initial offerings in the NoSQL space. In BigTable there was a simple data model that consisted of rows with columns and column groups. All operations on a row were atomic, and BigTable was the perfect match for some of the huge data problems that Google had to solve. Google Earth, Google Analytics, Personalized Search: all of these applications had to juggle petabytes of data using something a step up from the filesystem that would allow applications to work with data at scale. BigTable was all about "row mutations" and "scanners," and if you read between the lines of the BigTable paper in 2006 (*http://bit.ly/1dpvuTe*), not everyone was a fan of the access pattern for BigTable:

> Given the unusual interface to BigTable, an interesting question is how difficult it has been for our users to adapt to using it. New users are sometimes uncertain of how to best use the BigTable interface, **particularly if they are accustomed to using relational databases that support general-purpose transactions.** Nevertheless, the fact that many Google products successfully use BigTable demonstrates that our design works well in practice. [Emphasis added.]

My translation: "We think BigTable works for everything, but the AdWords group isn't convinced so they're still using MySQL."

Enter Megastore

A few years after Big Table, Megastore (*http://bit.ly/1al6cv5*) was created by what seems to be a completely separate team. Megastore was Google's internal reaction to BigTable, a sort of in-between SQL and NoSQL built atop BigTable. Here's the rationale behind Megastore from the Megastore paper (*http://bit.ly/1al6cv5*) (my emphasis included):

> "NoSQL datastores such as Google's BigTable, Apache Hadoop's HBase, or Facebook's Cassandra are highly scalable, but their **limited API and loose consistency models complicate application development.** Replicating data across distant data centers while providing low latency is challenging, as is guaranteeing a consistent view of replicated data, **especially during faults.**

Reading between the lines here, this strikes me as: "Yes, BigTable scales, but it's difficult to work with and we've had some annoying downtime because replication is a challenge." Megastore, like Spanner after it, made use of Paxos and also had a similar hierarchical data model (although not exactly the same). From the Megastore paper (*http://bit.ly/1al6cv5*):

> Megastore tables are either entity group root tables or child tables. Each child table must declare a single distinguished foreign key referencing a root table...Thus each child entity references a particular entity in its root table (called the root entity). An entity group consists of a root entity along with all entities in child tables that reference it.

There's another excerpt from the Megastore paper that foreshadows the weakness of this approach. While transactions were supported, they were discouraged. Here's the excerpt:

> Megastore supports two-phase commit for atomic updates across entity groups. Since these transactions have much higher latency and increase the risk of contention, we generally discourage applications from using the feature in favor of queues. Nevertheless, they can be useful in simplifying application code for unique secondary key enforcement.

This quote stands out knowing what we know now about the motivation to create Spanner. While Megastore provided transactions, it appears that using them created massive latency, inefficiency, and contention. In other words, and I'm reading between the lines again,

"Megastore supports transactions, but don't use them; they will ruin performance." It should also be noted that some of the applications that are using Megastore are the same applications that experienced widespread downtime a few years ago—Gmail among them (*http://bit.ly/1dpvvGK*).

If you remember Google's public explanation for day-long problems with Gmail, it was the combination of a loss of a single data center coupled with problems in replication. My guess is that the very public problems from years ago triggered an investment in the development of Spanner. There was an incentive to find a solution that could ensure consistency among data centers without having to worry about a separate replication process. There was also continued pressure to get AdWords off of the franken-MySQL deployment that is referenced in the Spanner paper.

Hey, Need Some Continent-Wide ACID? Here's Spanner

If I'm reading the author list correctly, the Spanner paper appears to be a merger of two separate teams. The BigTable authors and the Megastore authors collaborated to create what is likely the successor to BigTable. Spanner takes some ideas from Megastore, building upon the hierarchical schema with root tables (in Spanner directories), it also redefines the low-level approach to storage. Where Megastore relies on BigTable for storage, Spanner takes responsibility for storage, defining a new B-tree-based approach to storing segmented keys and data that correspond to these "schematized semi-relational tables."

The BigTable team defined an approach to persistence that could scale in 2006, in 2009–2010 the Megastore team built a solution with a more natural data model and transaction support atop BigTable. Megastore, while satisfying an internal need for storage with structure, still presented significant challenges because truly distributed transactions were only possible with significant latency penalties. So what does Google do? They solve the fundamental problem—time uncertainty. They retool the underlying approach to BigTable tablets to store hierarchical, semi-relational data.

Did Google Just Prove an Entire Industry Wrong?

My read of this paper is that Google just proved a lot of NoSQL proponents wrong. Most of the rationale I read for switching to NoSQL is the inability to support both transactions and horizontally scaled, distributed systems. Like the BigTable paper, this Spanner paper will take some time to percolate through the industry. We've been playing catch up with Google since the early part of the last decade, and it looks like we'll be playing catch up for some time because Google just proved that you can scale the relational database horizontally and have consistent transactions across a continent.

So the next time someone tells you that the relational database is "over" or "dead," point them at the Spanner paper.

QFS Improves Performance of Hadoop Filesystem

Open source file system by Quantcast

By Andy Oram (*http://bit.ly/1al6d2a*)

A new open source filesystem that takes up half the space and runs significantly faster than HDFS is now available for Hadoop, thanks to a firm named Quantcast (*http://bit.ly/1dpvuCB*). Their Quantcast File System (QFS) is being released today under an Apache 2 license and is immediately available for free download on GitHub (*http://bit.ly/1al6ban*).

If you're one of those grumblers (I admit to it) who complains about the widespread tracking of web users for marketing purposes, you can pause to thank Quantcast for funding this significant advance out of their own pockets as a big data company in the advertising space. They started using Hadoop when they launched in 2006, storing a terabyte of data on web audiences each day. Now, using QFS as their primary data store, they add 40 terabytes of new data and their daily Hadoop processing can exceed 20 petabytes.

As they grew, Quantcast tweaked and enhanced the various tools in the Hadoop chain. In 2008, they adopted the Kosmos File System (KFS) and hired its lead developer, Sriram Rao. After much upgrading for reliability, scalability, manageability, they are now releasing the filesystem to the public as QFS. They hope to see other large-scale Hadoop users evaluate and adopt it for their own big data processing needs and collaborate on its ongoing development. The source code is available on GitHub, as well as prebuilt binaries for several popular versions of Linux.

The key enhancement to QFS seemed simple in retrospect, but tricky to implement. Standard HDFS achieves fault tolerance by storing three copies of each file; in contrast, QFS uses a technique called Reed-Solomon encoding, which has been in wide use since the 1980s in products such as CDs and DVDs.

According to Jim Kelly, vice president of R&D at Quantcast, HDFS's optimization approach was well chosen when it was invented. Networks were relatively slow, so data locality was important, and HDFS tried to store a complete copy of each file on the node most likely to access it. But in intervening years, networks have grown tenfold in speed, leaving disks as the major performance bottleneck, so it's now possible to achieve better performance, fault tolerance, and disk space efficiency by distributing data more widely.

The form of Reed-Solomon encoding used in QFS stores redundant data in nine places and is able to reconstruct the file from any six of these stripes. Whereas HDFS could lose a file if the three disks hosting it happen to fail, QFS is more robust.

More importantly, Reed-Solomon adds only 50% to the size of the data stored, making it twice as efficient as HDFS in terms of storage space, which also has ripple effects in savings on servers, power, cooling, and more.

Furthermore, the technique increases performance: writes are faster, because only half as much data needs to be written, and reads are faster, because every read is done by six drives working in parallel. Quantcast's benchmarks of Hadoop jobs using HDFS and QFS show a 47% performance improvement in reads over HDFS, and a 75% improvement in writes.

QFS is also a bit more efficient because it is written in C++ instead of Java. Hadoop uses existing JNI binds to communicate with it.

Quantcast expects QFS to be of most interest to established Hadoop shops processing enough data that cost-efficient use of hardware is a significant concern. Smaller environments, those new to Hadoop, or those needing specific HDFS features will probably find HDFS a better fit. They have done intensive testing internally, running QFS in production for over a year, so now it's time to see how the code holds up in a wider public test.

Seven Reasons Why I Like Spark

Spark is becoming a key part of a big data toolkit.

By Ben Lorica (*http://bit.ly/1dptMRz*)

A large portion of this week's Amp Camp (*http://bit.ly/1al6bqS*) at UC Berkeley is devoted to an introduction to Spark (*http://bit.ly/1dpvy5d*)–an open source, in-memory, cluster computing framework. After playing with Spark over the last month, I've come to consider it a key part of my big data toolkit. Here's why:

Hadoop integration
    Spark can work with files stored in HDFS, an important feature given the amount of investment in the Hadoop ecosystem. Getting Spark to work with MapR (*http://bit.ly/1al6bHu*) is straightforward.

The Spark interactive shell
    Spark is written in Scala, and has it's own version of the Scala interpreter. I find this extremely convenient for testing short snippets of code.

The Spark analytic suite
    Spark comes with tools for interactive query analysis (Shark), large-scale graph processing and analysis (*http://bit.ly/14qThku*) (Bagel), and real-time analysis (Spark Streaming). Rather than having to mix and match a set of tools (e.g., Hive, Hadoop, Mahout, S4/Storm), you only have to learn one programming paradigm. For SQL enthusiasts, the added bonus is that Shark tends to run faster than Hive. If you want to run Spark in the cloud, there are a set of EC2 scripts (*http://bit.ly/1al6e67*) available.

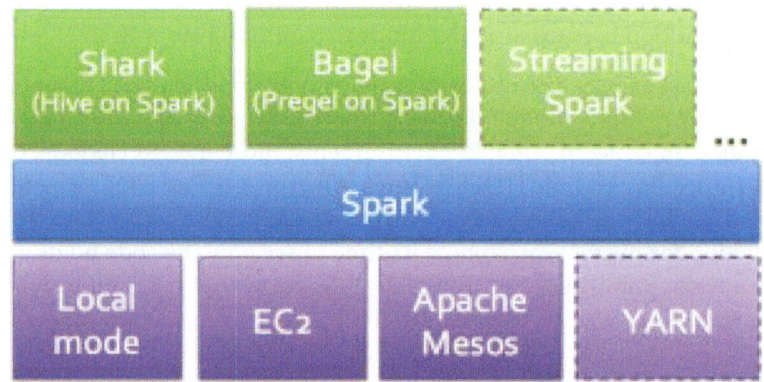

(Figure courtesy of Matei Zaharia (*http://bit.ly/1dpvx1f*).)

Resilient distributed data sets (RDDs)
RDDs (*http://bit.ly/1al6cet*) are *distributed objects* that can be cached in memory across a cluster of compute nodes. They are the fundamental data objects used in Spark. The crucial thing is that fault tolerance is built in: RDDs are *automatically* rebuilt if something goes wrong. If you need to test something out, RDDs can even be used interactively from the Spark interactive shell.

Distributed operators
Aside from Map and Reduce, there are many other operators one can use on RDDs (*http://bit.ly/1dpvxhT*). Once I familiarized myself with how they work, I began converting a few basic machine-learning and data processing algorithms into this framework.

Once You Get Past the Learning Curve … Iterative Programs

It takes some effort to become productive in anything, and Spark is no exception. I was a complete Scala newbie, so I first had to get comfortable with a new language (apparently, they like underscores: see here (*http://slidesha.re/1al6eDd*), here (*http://bit.ly/1dpvAdA*), and here (*http://bit.ly/1al6fqJ*)). Beyond Scala, one can use Shark (SQL on Spark), and relatively new Java and Python API's.

You can use the examples that come with Spark (*http://bit.ly/1dpvzq3*) to get started, but I found the essential thing is to get comfortable with the built-in distributed operators. Once I learned RDDs and the operators, I started writing iterative programs to implement a few machine-learning and data processing algorithms. (Since Spark distributes and caches data in memory, you can write pretty fast machine-learning programs on massive data sets.)

It's Already Used in Production

Is anyone *really* using Spark? While the list of companies is still small, judging from the size of the SF Spark Meetup (*http://bit.ly/1al6i5P*) and Amp Camp (*http://bit.ly/1al6bqS*), I expect many more companies to start deploying Spark. (If you're in the San Francisco Bay Area, we are starting a new Distributed Data Processing Meetup (*http://bit.ly/1al6gek*) with Airbnb, and Spark is one of the topics we'll cover.)

Update (8/23/2012)

Here's another important reason to like Spark–at 14,000 lines of code, it's much simpler than other software used for big data.

The Spark Codebase Is Small, Extensible, and Hackable.

Matei's last presentation at Amp Camp (*http://bit.ly/1dpvCSu*) included the diagram below (LOC = lines of code).

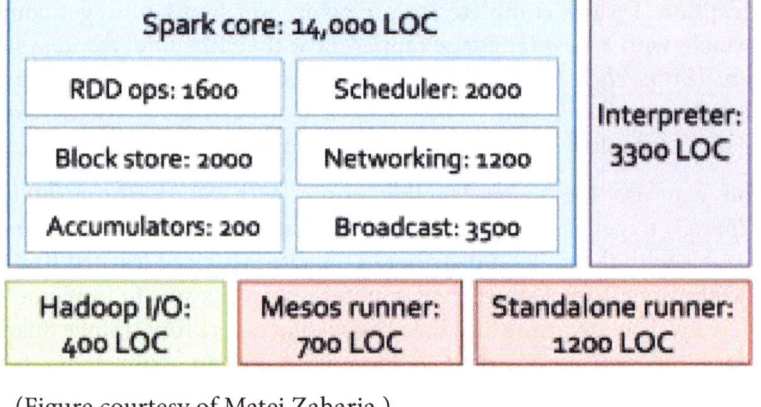

(Figure courtesy of Matei Zaharia.)

Changing Definitions

What is a data scientist? Why do we need people who know R? How much do we expect consumers to understand statistics? What are the ethical ramifications and unintended consequences of big data? If you work with big data, if it is your job to manage this data or to explore it with the tools we've discussed on the Strata blog, you've either asked these questions or had these questions asked of you. Nine years after the development of BigTable at Google and eight years after the invention of Hadoop, the ecosystems of developers, data analysts, and business people who depend on big data are starting to discuss the reasons why we're collecting data and the ways in which we think about what we're doing.

The posts in this section reflect the robust discussion happening at Strata about the definition of data scientists and the various roles such a position plays at different companies. We're still figuring out the answers to such questions as Kolegraff asks in his post "Do You Need a Data Scientist?" on page 70. We're also still considering issues of big data skepticism, such as those raised in Mike Loukides' post "Leading Indicators" on page 76.

This chapter also addresses times during this year when the fundamental assumption and definitions of big data have been questioned. Whatever big data really is, it is clear that the conferences and events Strata assembles are popular with an evolving crowd of both business and technology professionals. It is also clear that the movement is producing real results outside the handful of technology companies that started it. It is clear, though, that the "profession" of big data and data analysis is still in flux. Will we still be publishing a "big data" book in 2023? If so, to whom will it be targeted? Will the current technically focused content still be the content that is relevant to individuals with the job title "data scientist," or will these terms seem antiquated?

Some of our writers struck an optimistic tone about the movement, but a pessimistic tone about the ultimate result. This reflects the tension that characterized the year. Take this quote from Alistair Croll's "Three Kinds of Big Data" on page 105:

> That's my bet for the next three years, given the molasses of market confusion, vendor promises, and unrealistic expectations we're about to contend with. Will big data change the world? Absolutely. Will it be able to defy the usual cycle of earnest adoption, crushing disappointment, and eventual rebirth all technologies must travel? Certainly not.

Do You Need a Data Scientist?

Data science is hard, but it isn't dark magic

By Nick Kolegraff (*http://oreil.ly/1al6iCX*)

The question "do you need a data scientist?" came up a lot when I was a management consultant for a global firm that successfully incubated data science within a few enterprise organizations. It's hard. The discussion is hard and the culture clash for data scientists is hard. Many approach data science as some dark magic from Hogwarts. It's not. Investigating a hypothesis takes time. Spontaneously generating data and building a model against that data doesn't work. Understanding who you need and how they will fit into your organization is challenging. Where do we put them? Who do they interact with? What is the handoff? Who do we structure around the project? How do you execute a project? Even better, how do we make *money*? Yet, before we go there, perhaps we should step back a bit and think of this as a strategic question. Because maybe you do need a data scientist and maybe you don't.

If you are thinking about whether or not you need a data scientist, then here are some questions and insights to consider.

How Accessible Is Your Data?

- Algorithms are not the problem. Understanding what data goes into those algorithms is the crux of the issue. This requires accessible data.

- There are many access patterns in data science. These patterns include discovery, development, deployment, and maintenance. Getting to an infrastructure and data lifecycle that supports these patterns takes time.
- Data scientists ask a lot of questions about data. Asking questions on raw data is hard and time intensive. It is expensive to pay a data scientist to ask questions on raw data when you are doing an insights-driven project. It is probably best to enhance your calm and bring them on board when your data is ready for witchcraft and wizardry.
- Focus on getting accessible quality data and solid reporting. Then worry about data science. You'll save money and efficiency.

How versus why

- If you start with data science and ask how you do it rather than why you need it, you end up solving a problem for the wrong use case. For example, you may end up focusing on scale and then find out what you needed was effective sampling techniques.
- If you solve for why, how becomes easy.

Product or project?

- Are you making a product or doing a six-month project?
- Is the project being reused?
- A product that has a point of failure on a data pipeline is different from a project that needs the output of a data pipeline.
- A data scientist can certainly do a project and get insights; building an infrastructure that empowers a group of data scientists to drive insights takes a product mindset. Data reusability and accessibility are key.
- Data scientists are product people. You can sell a product for a long time. It is hard to justify ROI on a data scientist for a short-term project that isn't likely to be reused.

I firmly believe that everyone in the enterprise needs or will need data science at some point. Yet, finding a relevant product that requires data science is the hard part. Statistics and predictive modeling are not new.

Throw in ad hoc innovative culture, scale, and reusable data pipelines all feeding some user application and you might have data science. Maybe the question isn't *"Do you need a data scientist?"* but rather, *"Are you doing something right now that warrants data science?"*

Another Serving of Data Skepticism

By Mike Loukides (*http://bit.ly/1dpvD99*)

I was thrilled to receive an invitation to a new meetup: the NYC Data Skeptics Meetup (*http://bit.ly/1al6iTs*). If you're in the New York area, and you're interested in seeing data used honestly, stop by!

That announcement pushed me to write another post about data skepticism. The past few days, I've seen a resurgence of the slogan that correlation is as good as causation, if you have enough data. And I'm worried. (And I'm not vain enough to think it's a response to my first post about skepticism; it's more likely an effect of Cukier's book (*http://amzn.to/1dpvC51*).) There's a fundamental difference between correlation and causation. Correlation is a two-headed arrow: you can't tell in which direction it flows. Causation is a single-headed arrow: A causes B, not vice versa, at least in a universe that's subject to entropy.

Let's do some thought experiments—unfortunately, totally devoid of data. But I don't think we need data to get to the core of the problem. Think of the classic false correlation (when teaching logic, also used as an example of a false syllogism): there's a strong correlation between people who eat pickles and people who die. Well, yeah. We laugh. But let's take this a step further: correlation is a double-headed arrow. So not only does this poor logic imply that we can reduce the death rate by preventing people from eating pickles, it also implies that we can harm the chemical companies that produce vinegar by preventing people from dying. And here we see what's really happening: to remove one head of the double-headed arrow, we use common sense to choose between two stories: one that's merely silly, and another that's so ludicrous we never even think about it. Seems to work here (for a very limited value of "work"); but if I've learned one thing, it's that good old common sense is frequently neither common nor sensible. For more realistic correlations, it certainly seems ironic that we're doing all this data analysis just to end up relying on common sense.

Now let's look at something equally hypothetical that isn't silly. A drug is correlated with reduced risk of death due to heart failure. Good thing, right? Yes—but why? What if the drug has nothing to do with heart failure, but is really an anti-depressant that makes you feel better about yourself so you exercise more? If you're in the "correlation is as good as causation" club, doesn't make a difference: you win either way. Except that, if the key is really exercise, there might be much better ways to achieve the same result. Certainly much cheaper, since the drug industry will no doubt price the pills at $100 each. (Tangent: I once saw a truck drive up to an orthopedist's office and deliver Vioxx samples with a street value probably in the millions…) It's possible, given some really interesting work being done on the placebo effect (*http://bit.ly/1al6hir*), that a properly administered sugar pill will make the patient feel better and exercise, yielding the same result. (Though it's possible that sugar pills only work as placebos if they're expensive.) I think we'd like to know, rather than just saying that correlation is just as good as causation, if you have a lot of data.

Perhaps I haven't gone far enough: with enough data, and enough dimensions to the data, it would be possible to detect the correlations between the drug, psychological state, exercise, and heart disease. But that's not the point. First, if correlation really is as good as causation, why bother? Second, to analyze data, you have to collect it. And before you collect it, you have to decide what to collect. Data is socially constructed (I promise, this will be the subject of another post), and the data you don't decide to collect doesn't exist. Decisions about what data to collect are almost always driven by the stories we want to tell. You can have petabytes of data, but if it isn't the right data, if it's data that's been biased by preconceived notions of what's important, you're going to be misled. Indeed, any researcher knows that huge data sets tend to create spurious correlations (*http://wrd.cm/1dpvDGb*).

Causation has its own problems, not the least of which is that it's impossible to prove. Unfortunately, that's the way the world works. But thinking about cause and how events relate to each other helps us to be more critical about the correlations we discover. As humans, we're storytellers, and an important part of data work is building a story around the data (*http://bit.ly/1al6kup*). Mere correlations arising from a gigantic pool of data aren't enough to satisfy us. But there are good stories and bad ones, and just as it's possible to be careful in designing your experiments, it's possible to be careful and ethical in the stories you tell with your data. Those stories may be the closest we ever get to an understanding of cause; but we have to realize that they're just stories, that they're provisional, and that better evidence (which may just be correlations) may force us to retell our stories at any moment. Correlation is as good as causation is just an excuse for intellectual sloppiness; it's an excuse to replace thought with an odd kind of "common sense," and to shut down the discussion that leads to good stories and understanding.

A Different Take on Data Skepticism

Our tools should make common cases easy and safe, but that's not the reality today

By Beau Cronin (*http://oreil.ly/1dpvEd4*)

Recently, the Mathbabe (aka Cathy O'Neil (*http://bit.ly/1al6kuG*)) vented some frustration (*http://bit.ly/1dpvEtP*) about the pitfalls in applying even simple machine-learning (ML) methods like *k*-nearest neighbors. As data science is democratized, she worries that naive practitioners will shoot themselves in the foot because these tools can offer very misleading results. Maybe data science is best left to the pros? Mike Loukides picked up this thread (*http://oreil.ly/1al6kL9*), calling for healthy skepticism in our approach to data and implicitly cautioning against a "cargo cult" approach in which data collection and analysis methods are blindly copied from previous efforts without sufficient attempts to understand their potential biases and shortcomings.

Well, arguing against greater understanding of the methods we apply is like arguing against motherhood and apple pie, and Cathy and Mike are spot on in their diagnoses of the current situation. And yet…

There is so much value to be gained if we can put the power of learning, inference, and prediction methods into the hands of more developers and domain experts. But how can we avoid the pitfalls that Cathy and Mike are rightly concerned about? If a seemingly simple method like *k*-nearest neighbors classification is dangerous in unskilled hands (and it certainly is), then what hope is there? Well, I would argue that all ML methods are not created equal with regard to their safety. In fact, it is exactly some of the simplest (and most widely used) methods that are the most dangerous.

Why? Because these methods have lots of hidden assumptions. Well, maybe the assumptions aren't so much hidden as nodded-at-but-rarely-questioned. A good analogy might be jumping to the sentencing phase of a criminal trial without first assessing guilt: asking "What is the punishment that best fits this crime?" before asking "Did the defendant actually commit a crime? And if so, which one?" As another example of a simple-yet-dangerous method, *k*-means clustering assumes a value for k, the number of clusters, even though there may not be a good way to divide the data into this many buckets. Maybe seven buckets provides a much more natural explanation than four. Or maybe the data, as observed, is truly undifferentiated and any effort to split it up will result in arbitrary and misleading distinctions. Shouldn't our methods ask these more fundamental questions as well?

So, which methods are better in this regard? In general, it's those that explore model *space* in addition to model *parameters*. In the case of *k*-means, for example, this would mean learning the number *k* in addition to the cluster assignment for each data point. For *k*-nearest neighbors, we could learn the number of exemplars to use and also the distance metric that provides the best explanation for the data. This multilevel approach might sound advanced, and it is true that these implementations are more complex. But complexity of implementation needn't correlate with *danger* (thanks in part to software engineering), and it's certainly not a sufficient reason to dismiss more robust methods.

I find the database analogy useful here: developers with only a foggy notion of database implementation routinely benefit from the expertise of the programmers who do understand these systems—i.e., the "professionals." How? Well, decades of experience—and lots of trial and error—have yielded good abstractions in this area. As a result, we can meaningfully talk about the database *layer* in our overall *stack*. Of course, these abstractions are leaky, like all others, and there are plenty of sharp edges remaining (and, some might argue, more being created every day with the explosion of NoSQL solutions). Nevertheless, my weekend-project webapp can store and query insane amounts of data —and I have no idea how to implement a B-tree (*http://bit.ly/ 1a1nFUz*).

For ML to have a similarly broad impact, I think the tools need to follow a similar path. We need to push ourselves away from the viewpoint that sees ML methods as a bag of tricks, with the right method chosen on a per-problem basis, success requiring a good deal of art, and evaluation mainly by artificial measures of accuracy at the expense of other considerations. Trustworthiness, robustness, and conservatism are just as important, and will have far more influence on the long-run impact of ML.

Will well-intentioned people still be able to lie to themselves? Sure, of course! Let alone the greedy or malicious actors that Cathy and Mike are also concerned about. But our tools should make the common cases easy and safe, and that's not the reality today.

Leading Indicators

By Mike Loukides (*http://bit.ly/1dpvD99*)

In a conversation with Q. Ethan McCallum (*http://bit.ly/1dpvIcV*) (who should be credited as co-author), we wondered how to evaluate data science groups. If you're looking at an organization's data science group from the outside, possibly as a potential employee, what can you use to evaluate it? It's not a simple problem under the best of conditions: you're not an insider, so you don't know the full story of how many projects it has tried, whether they have succeeded or failed, relations between the data group, management, and other departments, and all the other stuff you'd like to know but will never be told.

Our starting point was remote: Q. told me about Tyler Brulé's travel writing (*http://on.ft.com/1adjt8W*) for *Financial Times* (behind a paywall, unfortunately), in which he says that a club sandwich is a good proxy for hotel quality: you go into the restaurant and order a club sandwich. A club sandwich isn't hard to make: there's no secret recipe or technique that's going to make Hotel A's sandwich significantly better than B's. But it's easy to cut corners on ingredients and preparation. And if a hotel is cutting corners on their club sandwiches, they're probably cutting corners in other places.

This reminded me of when my daughter was in first grade, and we looked (briefly) at private schools. All the schools talked the same talk. But if you looked at classes, it was pretty clear that the quality of the music program was a proxy for the quality of the school. After all, it's easy to shortchange music, and both hard and expensive to do it right. Oddly enough, using the music program as a proxy for evaluating school quality has continued to work through middle school and (public) high school. It's the first thing to cut when the budget gets tight; and if a school has a good music program with excellent teachers, they're probably not shortchanging the kids elsewhere.

How does this connect to data science? What are the proxies that allow you to evaluate a data science program from the outside, on the information that you might be able to cull from company blogs, a job interview, or even a job posting? We came up with a few ideas:

- Are the data scientists simply human search engines, or do they have real projects that allow them to explore and be curious? If they have management support for learning what can be learned from the organization's data, and if management listens to what they discover, they're accomplishing something significant. If they're just playing Q&A with the company data, finding answers to specific questions without providing any insight, they're not really a data science group.

- Do the data scientists live in a silo, or are they connected with the rest of the company? In "Building Data Science Teams," (*http://oreil.ly/1aKXJwT*) DJ Patil wrote about the value of seating data scientists with designers, marketers, with the entire product group so that they don't do their work in isolation, and can bring their insights to bear on all aspects of the company.

- When the data scientists do a study, is the outcome predetermined by management? Is it OK to say "we don't have an answer" or to come up with a solution that management doesn't like? Granted, you aren't likely to be able to answer this question without insider information.

- What do job postings look like? Does the company have a mission and know what it's looking for, or are they asking for someone with a huge collection of skills, hoping that they will come in useful? That's a sign of data science cargo culting.

- Does management know what their tools are for, or have they just installed Hadoop because it's what the management magazines tell them to do? Can managers talk intelligently to data scientists?

- What sort of documentation does the group produce for its projects? Like a club sandwich, it's easy to shortchange documentation.

- Is the business built around the data? Or is the data science team an add-on to an existing company? A data science group can be integrated into an older company, but you have to ask a lot more questions; you have to worry a lot more about silos and management relations than you do in a company that is built around data from the start.

Coming up with these questions was an interesting thought experiment; we don't know whether it holds water, but we suspect it does. Any ideas and opinions?

Data's Missing Ingredient? Rhetoric

Arguments are the glue that connects data to decisions

By Max Shron (*http://oreil.ly/1al6nGE*)

Data is key to decision making. Yet we are rarely faced with a situation where things can be put in to such a clear logical form that we have no choice but to accept the force of evidence before us. In practice, we should always be weighing alternatives, looking for missed possibilities, and considering what else we need to figure out before we can proceed.

Arguments are the glue that connects data to decisions. And if we want good decisions to prevail, both as decision makers and as data scientists, we need to better understand how arguments function. We need to understand the best ways that arguments and data interact. The statistical tools we learn in classrooms are not sufficient alone to deal with the messiness of practical decision making.

Examples of this fill the headlines. You can see evidence of rigid decision making in how the American medical establishment decides what constitutes a valid study result. By custom and regulation, there is an official statistical breaking point for all studies. Below this point, a result will be acted upon. Above, it won't be. Cut and dry, but dangerously brittle.

The results can be deadly. Between 1999 and 2004, an estimated 60,000 people died from taking Vioxx, a painkiller marketed for arthritis. Evidence came to light early on that the drug increased the risk of heart attack. But because official decision making was based on a break point and not nuanced argument, the drug stayed on the market for years. Nuanced reasoning can save lives.

If this kind of procedure sounds familiar, it's probably because it's the dominant way that people use data across business, government, and academia. The numbers are up? The graph trends down? The slope is "significant"? Congratulations, according to the absurdly low standards that prevail in most places, you're bolding using data! Here is a gold star.

Thinking explicitly about arguing has traditionally been a skill of humanities professors, lawyers, and the occasional elder scientist. If data is going to be our new guiding light, then as data scientists, managers of data scientists, or people who want to better use data in pursuit of excellence in any field, we need to get more comfortable with the tools of arguments.

It's become common knowledge across business, the nonprofit sector, and academia that we are "swimming" in data, yet constantly "falling behind" on making good use of it. Depending on who you ask, the latest tools or newest techniques are the cure-all that we need to turn these raw facts into insights.

What's missing from all of these discussions is a hard look at how people actually move from data to decision. How does data compel someone to change their mind? Even more importantly, how does data compel someone to act differently?

This is an old question, and it has an old answer. The answer is rhetoric, though perhaps not the way that you may think of the word. The ancient Greeks understood that studying how and why people came to be convinced of things was a worthwhile field in and of itself. Rhetoric is the study of arguments presented by one person to another. It has seen a resurgence in the last fifty years, after a quiet period stretching from the 17th century onward. Dialectic, its sibling, is the study of how arguments are conducted between two people holding different viewpoints.

Historically, "rhetoric" didn't have the connotation of flashy presentation (which is how the word is often used today). Instead, traditionally rhetoric has been the study of all aspects of argumentation: inventing arguments, arranging arguments, understanding the goals of an argument, and, ultimately, making an intelligent presentation.

Understanding arguments helps us think up new ideas, helps us weigh possibilities against each other, and helps us think critically about what people are trying to convince us to say and do. Arguments are everywhere. Every time you play around with a spreadsheet, or make an exploratory graph, or do some quick tabulations, there is an argument, or a fragment of an argument, at play. All arguments have structure. Understanding that structure is powerful.

Data Skepticism

If data scientists aren't skeptical about how they use and analyze data, who will be?

By Mike Loukides (*http://bit.ly/1dpvD99*)

A couple of months ago, I wrote that big data is heading toward the trough of a hype curve (*http://oreil.ly/1al6nX9*) as a result of oversized hype and promises. That's certainly true. I see more expressions of skepticism about the value of data every day. Some of the skepticism is a reaction against the hype; a lot of it arises from ignorance, and it has the same smell as the rich history of science denial from the tobacco industry (and probably much earlier) onward.

But there's another thread of data skepticism that's profoundly important. On her MathBabe blog, Cathy O'Neil has written several articles about lying with data (*http://bit.ly/1dpvHpj*)—about intentionally developing models that don't work because it's possible to make more money from a bad model than a good one. (If you remember Mel Brooks' classic *The Producers* (*http://bit.ly/1al6ou8*), it's the same idea.) In a slightly different vein, Cathy argues that making machine learning simple (*http://bit.ly/1dpvEtP*) for nonexperts might not be in our best interests; it's easy to start believing answers because the computer told you so, without understanding why those answers might not correspond with reality.

I had a similar conversation with David Reiley (*http://bit.ly/1al6oup*), an economist at Google, who is working on experimental design in social sciences. Heavily paraphrasing our conversation, he said that it was all too easy to think you have plenty of data, when in fact you have the wrong data, data that's filled with biases that lead to misleading conclusions. As Reiley points out (*http://bit.ly/1dpvHWx*), "the population of people who sees a particular ad may be very different from the population who does not see an ad"; yet many data-driven studies of advertising effectiveness don't take this bias into account. The idea that there are limitations to data, even very big data, doesn't contradict Google's mantra that more data is better than smarter algorithms; it does mean that even when you have unlimited data, you have to be very careful about the conclusions you draw from that data. It is in conflict with the all-too-common idea that, if you have lots and lots of data, correlation is as good as causation.

Skepticism about data is normal, and it's a good thing. If I had to give a one line definition of science, it might be something like "organized and methodical skepticism based on evidence." So, if we really want to do data science, it has to be done by incorporating skepticism. And here's the key: data scientists have to own that skepticism. Data scientists have to be the biggest skeptics. Data scientists have to be skeptical about models, they have to be skeptical about overfitting, and they have to be skeptical about whether we're asking the right questions. They have to be skeptical about how data is collected, whether that data is unbiased, and whether that data—even if there's an inconceivably large amount of it—is sufficient to give you a meaningful result.

Because the bottom line is: if we're not skeptical about how we use and analyze data, who will be? That's not a pretty thought.

On the Importance of Imagination in Data Science

Strata community profile on Amy Heineike, Director of Mathematics.

By Janaya Williams (*http://bit.ly/1al6oKV*)

According to Amy Heineike (*http://bit.ly/1dpvKSe*), the Director of Mathematics at Quid (*http://bit.ly/1al6phO*), there's nothing like having a fresh dataset in R (*http://bit.ly/1dpvKBG*) and knowing how to use it. "You can add a few lines of code and discover all kinds of interesting information," Heineike says. "One question leads to another, you get into a flow, and you can have an amazing exploration."

Heineike started working with data several years ago at a consultancy in London, where "playing around" with data shed light on the impact of social networks on government policies. Part of her job was figuring out what types of data to use in order to find solutions to crucial problems, from public transportation to obesity. Her day-to-day work at Quid entails working with new data sets, prototyping analytics, and collaborating with an engineering team to improve data analysis and bring products into production.

At Strata Santa Clara (*http://oreil.ly/1al6pyl*), she spoke with me about the importance of imagination in data science, using visualizations as a tool, and how data teams can work better together.

Can you talk a bit about how the team at Quid uses maps and visualizations to explore data?

Amy Heineike: Because we are living so much of our lives online, more and more of our collective conversations are happening through blog posts, social media, news articles, web pages, or government filings that end up online. This includes lots of really messy, unstructured, interesting, rich material.

A lot of the tools that are commonly available to systematically evaluate content online makes the process painful and difficult. Our challenge is to make visual maps of the data that you would otherwise have to consume by reading every single piece of it. Our maps aren't geographic or spatial, they're topical. It's not latitude and longitude that you point to on the maps, it's an idea.

It's well known that math is a crucial competence in the data science field. What other attributes do you think data scientists need to be effective?

Amy Heineike: I think it's important that people in this kind of role care a lot about what they are building. They should have the imagination to think about the person who might use what they are building and what they might want to achieve.

In that sense, data scientists are a bit like product managers. Product managers figure out what features should go into a website or software tool. Data science is similar to that, but when you're thinking analytically, the question is, "Can I really get data that can build this?" and "Does the data support whatever it is I want to build?" Being able to see how things fit together is really important.

It's also the case that data is almost inevitably messy and hard to work with. And so learning how to look at data and understand the shape of it is important. Are there weird artifacts in the data? Or issues that you need to clean up? Are there strange things in the data that actually turn out to be the most interesting things?

I think the real magic comes from being able to realize that a product that you want to make, something that you want to build, could actually be made from either data that you have lying around, or data that you can fetch.

What tools do you use?

Amy Heineike: At Quid, we built a whole stack that starts off by pulling in big data sets that are going to be really important for answering big questions. The news, information about startup companies, basically anything we can grab from online and process. So we have a platform for sucking that in, and that's using several different tools and making use of different APIs.

We then have a platform for storing this data and indexing it, so we make use of a lot of elastic search at this point internally, to be able to access all the data.

Then we have the analytics engine and visualizations tools. There are actually a lot of bits to that. We use Python extensively and we've been playing around with a couple of different technologies on the visualization side. I used to use R extensively, but not so much anymore, which makes me sad because it's fun!

What capabilities are missing from the tools that you use? Are there instances where the tools that are available to you fall short of what you need them to do?

Amy Heineike: Even with tools that are relatively straightforward like R and Python, there is a pretty steep learning curve before you arrive at what's possible. What this means is that you could specialize in using the tools, but don't have much time to spend with the people who are using what you built. Or you spend a lot of time with people who are using what you built, and you don't have enough time to master the tools. So, I think that's one challenge.

At Quid, one of the reasons we like the idea of mapping and putting data in a format where people can come and explore it is that they don't have to touch Python, they don't have to worry about where the data came from, and they don't have to clean it up. People are able to just participate and ask a lot of questions.

Why? Why? Why!

A lesson for data science teams.

By Dean Malmgren (*http://oreil.ly/1dpvLW5*) and Mike Stringer (*http://oreil.ly/1al6q5j*)

The other day we had a conversation with a bespectacled senior data scientist at another organization (named X to protect the innocent). The conversation went something like the comic shown here.

Many of us have had similar conversations with people like X, and many of us have even been X before. Data scientists, being curious individuals, enjoy working on problems for the sake of doing something interesting, fun, technically challenging, or because their boss heard about "big data" in the *Wall Street Journal*. These reasons are all distinctly different from trying to solve an important problem.

This can be daunting for data scientists, because some important problems don't actually need a data scientist to solve. It is increasingly the case, however, that data can be used as an extraordinarily valuable resource to help solve age-old, time-tested business problems in innovative ways. Operations? Product development? Strategy? Human resources? Chances are that there are some data out there now, or that you can collect, that can help change your organization or drive an exciting new product.

To tap this increasingly abundant "natural" resource, however, a data science team must:

- Learn from business domain experts about real problems
- Think creatively about *if* and how data can be used as part of a solution
- Focus on problems that actually improve the business

Going in any different order is a recipe for disillusionment about big data's true potential. Starting with a real problem instead of starting with some interesting dataset often leads data scientists down a completely different—and much more fruitful—path.

Case in Point

As an example from our work at Datascope Analytics (*http://bit.ly/1dpvMcJ*), in 2010, Brian Uzzi (*http://bit.ly/1al6qlR*) introduced us to Daegis (*http://bit.ly/1dpvMth*), a leading e-discovery (*http://bit.ly/1al6thy*) services provider. Our initial conversations centered around social network analysis and thinking about how we could use connections between people to further their business. Daegis' clients store tons of email records and we could have made some sexy network diagrams or any number of other exciting things. It would have been interesting! It would have been fun! It would have been, well, mostly worthless had we not asked one important question first:

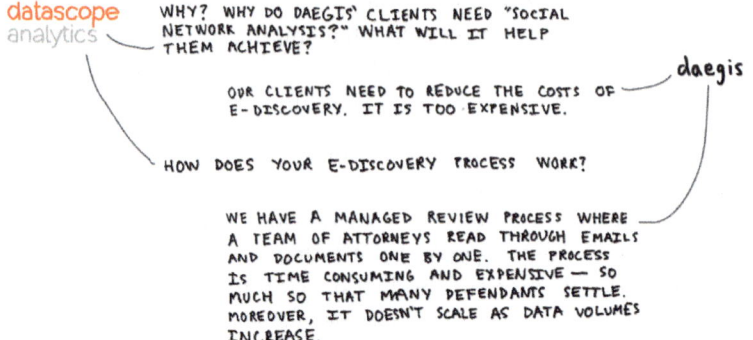

This is not necessarily a social network analysis problem. This is a classification problem where the goal is to accurately identify the small set of documents that are relevant to a lawsuit.

So we focused the first phase of our project with Daegis around building a quick prototype using data from the Text Retrieval Conference (TREC) (*http://bit.ly/1dpvOBi*) to demonstrate that our transductive learning algorithms (*http://bit.ly/1al6qT2*) could reduce the number of documents that needed to be reviewed by 80%–99%. This was huge! We were going to help Daegis gain a tremendous advantage and Daegis' clients would be able to defend themselves from frivolous lawsuits. +1 for the good guys.

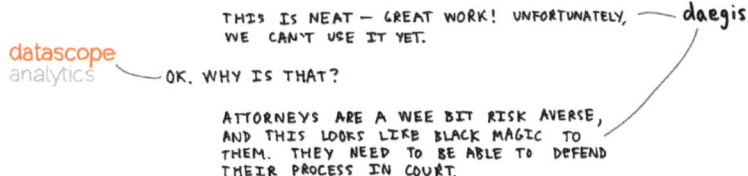

After several design iterations (see our Strata presentation (*http://oreil.ly/10legBC*) or slides (*http://slidesha.re/1al6r9v*) if you're interested), we arrived at some insights: what we developed needed to be educational, transparent, and understandable. By the end, if you had to summarize the project, it would be closer to "educating attorneys about information retrieval" than "social network analysis." The final result is a product that Daegis sells under the name Acumen (*http://bit.ly/1dpvQcg*) (subtle hint for attorneys out there: you should use it!).

The Take-Home Message

This case illustrates a lesson for data scientists: ask why first!

Be ready. The answers to this deceptively simple question may surprise you, take you into challenging uncharted territory, and inspire you to think about problems in completely different ways.

Big Data Is Dead, Long Live Big Data: Thoughts Heading to Strata

The biggest problems will almost always be those for which the size of the data is part of the problem.

By Mike Loukides (*http://bit.ly/1dpvD99*)

A recent *VentureBeat* article argues that big data is dead (*http://bit.ly/1dpvPFe*). It's been killed by marketers. That's an understandable frustration (and a little ironic to read about it in that particular venue). As I said sarcastically the other day, "Put your big data in the cloud with a Hadoop."

You don't have to read much industry news to get the sense that big data is sliding into the trough of Gartner's hype curve. That's natural. Regardless of the technology, the trough of the hype cycle is driven by by a familiar set of causes: it's fed by over-aggressive marketing, the longing for a silver bullet that doesn't exist, and the desire to spout the newest buzzwords. All of these phenomena breed cynicism. Perhaps the most dangerous is the technologist who never understands the limitations of data, never understands what data isn't telling you, or never understands that if you ask the wrong questions, you'll certainly get the wrong answers.

Big data is not a term I'm particularly fond of. It's just data, regardless of the size. But I do like Roger Magoulas' definition (*http://oreil.ly/ 1al6ulI*) of "big data": big data is when the size of the data becomes part of the problem. I like that definition because it scales. It was meaningful in 1960, when big data was a couple of megabytes. It will be meaningful in 2030, when we all have petabyte laptops, or eyeglasses connected directly to Google's yottabyte cloud. It's not convenient for marketing, I admit; today's "Big Data!!! With Hadoop And Other Essential Nutrients Added" is tomorrow's "not so big data, small data actually." Marketing, for better or for worse, will deal.

Whether or not Moore's Law continues indefinitely, the real importance of the amazing increase in computing power over the last six decades isn't that things have gotten faster; it's that the size of the problems we can solve has gotten much, much larger. Or as Chris Gaun just wrote, big data is leading scientists to ask bigger questions (*http:// bit.ly/1dpvPVS*). We've been a little too focused on Amdahl's law, about making computing faster, and not focused enough on the reverse: how big a problem can you solve in a given time, given finite resources? Modern astronomy, physics, and genetics are all inconceivable without really big data, and I mean big on a scale that dwarfs Amazon's inventory database. At the edges of research, data is, and always will be, part of the problem. Perhaps even the biggest part of the problem.

In the next year, we'll slog through the cynicism that's a natural outcome of the hype cycle. But I'm not worrying about cynicism. Data isn't like Java, or Rails, or any of a million other technologies; data has been with us since before computers were invented, and it will still be with us when we move onto whatever comes after digital computing. Data, and specifically big data, will always be at the edges of research and understanding. Whether we're mapping the brain (*http://bit.ly/ 1al6sdr*) or figuring out how the universe works (*http://bit.ly/ 1dpvSRC*), the biggest problems will almost always be the ones for which the size of the data is part of the problem. That's an invariant. That's why I'm excited about data.

Keep Your Data Science Efforts from Derailing

Preview of upcoming session at Strata Santa Clara.

By Marck Vaisman (*http://oreil.ly/1al6xOi*) and Sean Murphy (*http://oreil.ly/1dpvRwS*)

Is your organization considering embracing data science? If so, we would like to give you some helpful advice on organizational and technical issues to consider before you embark on any initiatives or consider hiring data scientists. Join us, Sean Murphy (*http://linkd.in/1al6vpB*) and Marck Vaisman (*http://linkd.in/1dpvTFe*), two Washington, D.C.-based data scientists and founding members of Data Community DC (*http://bit.ly/1al6vWR*), as we walk you through the trials and tribulations of practicing data scientists at our upcoming talk at Strata (*http://oreil.ly/1dpvTVF*).

We will discuss anecdotes and best practices, and finish by presenting the results of a survey we conducted last year to help understand the varieties of people, skills, and experiences that fall under the broad term of *data scientist*. We analyzed data from over 250 survey respondents, and are excited to share our findings, which will also be published soon by O'Reilly.

As is nicely summarized in the "Dark Side of Data Science" chapter of *The Bad Data Handbook* (*http://oreil.ly/RBfesg*) (Marck was a contributing author), we ask you–actually plead with you–to do the exact opposite of the following commandments:

I. Know Nothing About Thy Data

Please spend time understanding the nuances, intricacies, sources, and structure of your data. Trust us, this time is well spent. As they say, 80% of time spent on analytic tasks is munging, cleaning, transforming, etc. Don't let that be 90% or 95% of your effort.

II. Thou Shalt Provide Your Data Scientists with a Single Tool for All Tasks

No single tool can perform all possible data science tasks. Many different tools exist, and each tool has a specific purpose. Please provide data scientists access to the tools they need, and also the ability to configure them as needed–at least in research and development environments–without making them jump through hoops to do so.

III. Thou Shalt Analyze for Analysis' Sake Only

Some analytical exercises begin as open exploration; others begin with a specific question in mind, and end up answering a different one. Regardless, before you embark on an investigation, please have some idea of where you want to go. Please, don't do analysis just to say you are doing data science or because you have a lot of data. It's pointless.

IV. Thou Shalt Compartmentalize Learnings

We learned to share when we were children. Please share your learnings and findings within your organizations, as appropriate, to avoid duplicating work and wasting your time and ours.

V. Thou Shalt Expect Omnipotence from Data Scientists

This is, by far, our favorite commandment. We have run into numerous situations where organizations expect miracles because of the hype surrounding data science. Additionally, there seems to be a lack of awareness of the variety of skills that data scientists have, leading organizations to wasted time and effort when trying to find talent due to this misunderstanding.

As practitioners, we advocate that organizations and management please adjust their expectations accordingly, and that they should consider assembling a team whose members' broad skills have much overlap while their unique expertise does not. This will be further explored in the section discussing the survey results.

Your Analytics Talent Pool Is Not Made Up of Misanthropes

Tips for interacting with analytics colleagues.

By John Foreman (*http://oreil.ly/1dpvUsJ*)

To quote *Pride and Prejudice*, businesses have for many years "labored under the misapprehension" that their analytics talent was made up of misanthropes with neither the will nor the ability to communicate or work with others on strategic or creative business problems. These employees were meant to be kept in the basement out of sight, fed bad pizza, and pumped for spreadsheets to be interpreted in the sunny offices aboveground.

This perception is changing in industry as the big data phenomenon has elevated data science to a C-level priority. Suddenly folks once stereotyped by characters like Milton (*http://bit.ly/1al6zG0*) in *Office Space* are now "sexy" (*http://bit.ly/1dpvUZy*). The truth is there have always been well-rounded, articulate, friendly analytics professionals (they may just like *Battlestar* more than you), and now that analytics is an essential business function, personalities of all types are being attracted to practice the discipline.

Yet, despite this evolution both in talent and perception, many employees, both peers and managers, still treat their analytics counterparts in ways that erode effective analytics practice within an organization. The following sections cover five things to keep in mind as you interact with your analytics colleagues in the future.

#1: Analytics Is Not a One-Way Conversation

If you're going to ask a data scientist to study demand drivers or task your analysts to pull some aggregate data from the Hadoop cluster, try not to just "take the data and run." Analysts are humans, not a *layer* on top of your database so that MBAs can extract data. A data scientist is not a high-priced Mechanical Turk (*http://bit.ly/GzPZn4*).

Remember to communicate *why* you need the data you need. And later, when that data has come to some use, you should check back in with the analyst to let them know that their efforts did not go unwasted. I've seen organizations suffer from an analytics *throttling* effect where analysts will cease or slow down their work for a particular manager or peer, because they think the manager never does anything with the data. Maybe the manager doesn't, or maybe the manager just doesn't check back in to let the analyst know the outcome of their work.

Data scientists don't like data for its own sake. They like it for what it can *do*. So keep them in the loop.

#2: Give Credit Where Credit Is Due

Let's say your data scientist performs a study showing how "user agent of the customer visiting the website is predictive of conversion" or "we can target customers with product recommendations based on the purchases of their nearest neighbors." You then take this study and turn it into profit. The data scientist should receive some of the merit for having contributed to this work. It seems like common sense, but many businesses often think that crediting an analyst is like crediting the database they used. You wouldn't give credit to Hadoop for your great strategic idea, so why would you give it to this curmudgeonly analyst? Data doesn't become insight on its own. Someone had to craft those insights out of a pile of ugly transactional records, so give that person a pat on the back.

#3: Allow Analytics Professionals to Speak

Just because you may not have a knack for math, does not mean that your analyst isn't adept at communicating. Allowing an analyst to present their own work gives them a sense of ownership and belonging within the organization. Some analysts may not want to communicate. That's fine. But you'd be surprised how many would love to be part of the conversation if only they were given the chance. If they did the work, they might be able to better communicate the subtleties first-hand than an MBA could secondhand.

#4: Don't Bring in Your Analytics Talent Too Late

Often products and strategies are developed and launched by executives, managers, and marketers, and thrown in the wild long before someone thinks to ask the analyst, "Hey, how might we use data to make this product better? And how might we use the transactional data generated by this product to add value?" The earlier these questions get posed in the development cycle, the more impact analytics will have on the product in the long run.

Sure, you can't do data science until you have data, but a slight variation in how you sell, market, or design a product may mean the difference between useable data later on and worthless data. Design, marketing, operations—there are many important considerations at the beginning of any product's life. But don't let that stop you from bringing the data scientist into the high-level strategic meetings. They might be able to shape the product to make it more profitable through predictive modeling, forecasting, or optimization. You don't necessarily know what's analytically possible. But they do.

#5: Allow Your Scientists to Get Creative

When people think of creativity, they often think of the arts. But cognitively, there's a lot of similarity between fine art and abstract algebra (*http://bit.ly/1dpvUZP*). Analytics professionals need instructions, projects, and goals just like all other employees, but that doesn't mean they need to be told exactly what to do and how to do it 100% of the time.

Now that the world at large has realized products can be made from data or better sold through the judicious use of data, it's in your best interest to give your analytics professionals some flexibility to see what they can dream up. Ask them to think about what problems lying about the business could be solved through analytics. Maybe it's phone support prioritization, maybe it's optimizing your supply chain or using predictive modeling in recruiting, maybe it's revenue optimization through pricing—allow the analyst to think creatively about problems that seem outside their purview. It'll keep them interested and engaged in the business, rather than feeling marginalized and stuck-in-the-basement. A happy, engaged data scientist is a productive data scientist. And given how hard it is to recruit these professionals (they seem more like unicorns sometimes), hanging on to the talent you have is essential.

How Do You Become a Data Scientist? Well, It Depends

My obsession with data and user needs is now focused on the many paths toward data science.

By Ann Spencer (*http://bit.ly/1al6AtD*)

Over Thanksgiving, Richie (*http://bit.ly/1dpvWkq*) and Violet (*http://zd.net/1al6Ad4*) asked me if I preferred the iPhone or the Galaxy SIII. I have both. It is a long story. My response was, *"It depends."* Richie, who would probably bleed Apple if you cut him, was very unsatisfied with my answer. Violet was more diplomatic. Yet, it does depend. It depends on what the user wants to use the device for.

I say, *"It depends"* a lot in my life.

Both in the personal life and the work life…well, because it really is all one life isn't it? With my work over the past decade or so, I have been obsessive about being user focused. I spend a lot of time thinking about whom a product, feature, or service is for and how they will use it. Not how I want them to use it—how they want to use it and what problem they are trying to solve with it.

Before I joined O'Reilly, I was obsessively focused on the audience for my data analysis. C-level execs look for different kinds of insights than a director of engineering. A field sales rep looks for different insights than a software developer. Understanding more about who the user or audience was for a data project enabled me to map the insights to the user's role, their priorities, and how they wanted to use the data. Because, you know what isn't too great? When you spend a significant amount of time working on something that does not get used or is not what someone needed to help them in their job.

If there were a Data Analysis Anonymous support group, I'd bet that one of the top challenges discussed would be dealing with spending so much time, resources, and err…funding on unused data projects. This also crosses over to other roles within multiple industries. Just think about how many products, services, and additional features have been launched into the market and no one uses them. Each unused feature or product may represent hundreds, if not thousands, of human work hours. Wasted.

Since I've joined O'Reilly, a variation of the question "How do we help people become data scientists?" has come up every day. As the Strata editor, this is a question I should be thinking about every day…even at 12:48 AM staring at my ceiling or writing a Strata piece on a Saturday afternoon at a local cafe. My response often is, unsurprisingly, "It depends." There is no single path to becoming a data scientist. Saying that there is only one path to becoming a data scientist is like saying that all product directors started their careers with PhDs in computer science and electrical engineering. Ummmm. Yeah. So not the case.

At a very broad level, everyone interested in careers in data science will need to be familiar with some math, programming, tools, design, analysis…and wait for it…empathy. As in, empathy for the users of your data projects. Ooooh, I can already envision the hatertude that is going to fill my inbox with my empathy recommendation. Please feel free to bring it on. You can reach me at *pitchstrata@oreilly.com*.

Anyway.

How deep you need to go into each category depends on your background (quant, qualitative analyst, designer, software engineer, student, etc.) and what kind of work you want to do (open source, startups, government, corporate, etc.).

O'Reilly has a data science starter kit (*http://oreil.ly/1dpvYbZ*), which is a great bundle that provides insight into the broad technology categories. In the future, I'll provide additional suggestions on the types of resources users can reference to help them with their path toward learning more about data science, and if they want, becoming a data scientist. Within the Strata community site, I'll be seeking to answer questions like:

- "I'm currently a quant that works a lot with mySQL and am interested in data science. Now what?"
- "I am a software developer. Do I really need to learn any more math? Seriously?"
- "I'm currently a graphic designer. What should I learn about data science in order to bring additional meaning to my design?"

- "I think I want to get my PhD in math. Probably statistics. What else should I think about while I complete my studies if I want to be a data scientist when I grow up?"
- "I am a business intelligence analyst that works primarily with Excel. What other skills do I need to become a data scientist?"

These won't be the only questions. I'll also be seeking to provide insights to even more questions from many different types of users who are interested in data science. Keep a lookout for future postings from me and friends of O'Reilly that will provide more detailed recommendations. While I plan to cover quite a wide range of topics within the Strata community, insight into the multiple types of user-centric learning journeys needs to be addressed.

New Ethics for a New World

The biggest threat that a data-driven world presents is an ethical one.

By Alistair Croll (*http://bit.ly/1al6D8J*)

Since the first of our ancestors chipped stone into a weapon, technology has divided us. Seldom more than today, however: a connected, always-on society promises health, wisdom, and efficiency even as it threatens an end to privacy and the rise of prejudice masked as science.

On its surface, a data-driven society is more transparent, and makes better uses of its resources. By connecting human knowledge and mining it for insights, we can pinpoint problems before they become disasters, warding off disease and shining the harsh light of data on injustice and corruption. Data is making cities smarter, watering the grassroots, and improving the way we teach.

But for every accolade, there's a cautionary tale. It's easy to forget that data is merely a tool, and in the wrong hands, that tool can do powerful wrong. Data erodes our privacy. It predicts us, often with unerring accuracy—and treating those predictions as fact is a new, insidious form of prejudice. And it can collect the chaff of our digital lives, harvesting a picture of us we may not want others to know.

The big data movement isn't just about knowing more things. It's about a fundamental shift from scarcity to abundance. Most markets are defined by scarcity—the price of diamonds, or oil, or music. But when things become so cheap they're nearly free, a funny thing happens.

Consider the advent of steam power. Economist Stanley Jevons, in what's known as Jevons' Paradox (*http://bit.ly/1dpvX7J*), observed that as the efficiency of steam engines increased, coal consumption went up. That's not what was supposed to happen. Jevons realized that abundance creates new ways of using something. As steam became cheap, we found new ways of using it, which created demand.

The same thing is happening with data. A report that took a month to run is now just a few taps on a tablet. An unthinkably complex analysis of competitors is now a Google search. And the global distribution of multimedia content that once required a broadcast license is now an upload.

Big data is about reducing the cost of analyzing our world. The resulting abundance is triggering entirely new ways of using that data. Visualizations, interfaces, and ubiquitous data collection are increasingly important, because they feed the machine— and the machine is hungry.

The results are controversial. Journalists rely on global access to data, but also bring a new skepticism to their work, because facts are easy to manufacture. There's good evidence (*http://n.pr/1al6BNZ*) that we've never been as polarized, politically, as we are today—and data may be to blame. You can find evidence to support any conspiracy, expose any gaffe, or refute any position you dislike, but separating truth from mere data is a growing problem.

Perhaps the biggest threat that a data-driven world presents is an ethical one. Our social safety net is woven on uncertainty. We have welfare, insurance, and other institutions precisely because we can't tell what's going to happen—so we amortize that risk across shared resources. The better we are at predicting the future, the less we'll be willing to share our fates with others. And the more those predictions look like facts, the more justice looks like thoughtcrime.

The human race underwent a huge shift when we banded together into tribes, forming culture and morals to tie us to one another. As groups, we achieved great heights, building nations, conquering challenges, and exploring the unknown. If you were one of those tribesmen, it's unlikely you knew what was happening—it's only in hindsight that the shift from individual to group was radical.

We're in the middle of another, perhaps bigger shift, one that's taking us from physical beings to digital/physical hybrids. We're colonizing an online world, and just as our ancestors had to create covenants and moral guidelines to work as groups, so we have to new ethics, rights, and laws.

Those fighting for social change have their work cut out for them, because they're not just trying to find justice—they're helping to rewrite the ethical and moral guidelines for a nascent, always-on, data-driven species.

Why Big Data Is Big: The Digital Nervous System

Why we all need to understand and use big data.

By Edd Dumbill (*http://bit.ly/1dpvX7W*)

Where does all the data in big data (*http://oreil.ly/1al6Cld*) come from? And why isn't big data just a concern for companies such as Facebook and Google? The answer is that the web companies are the forerunners. Driven by social, mobile, and cloud technology, there is an important transition taking place, leading us all to the data-enabled world that those companies inhabit today.

From Exoskeleton to Nervous System

Until a few years ago, the main function of computer systems in society, and business in particular, was as a digital support system. Applications digitized existing real-world processes, such as word processing, payroll, and inventory. These systems had interfaces back out to the real world through stores, people, telephone, shipping and so on. The now-quaint phrase *paperless office* alludes to this transfer of pre-existing paper processes into the computer. These computer systems formed a *digital exoskeleton*, supporting a business in the real world.

The arrival of the Internet and Web has added a new dimension, bringing in an era of entirely digital business. Customer interaction, payments, and often product delivery can exist entirely within computer systems. Data doesn't just stay inside the exoskeleton any more, but is a key element in the operation. We're in an era where business and society are acquiring a *digital nervous system*.

As my sketch below shows, an organization with a digital nervous system is characterized by a large number of inflows and outflows of

.working, both internally and externally, in-
consequent complexity.

,hy big data is important. Techniques developed to
.ked, heterogeneous data acquired by massive web
. be our main tools as the rest of us transition to digital-
.ion. We see early examples of this, from catching fraud
.l transactions, to debugging and improving the hiring pro-
.IR (*http://oreil.ly/1dpvZfZ*); and almost everybody already
p. .tention to the massive flow of social network information con-
cerning them.

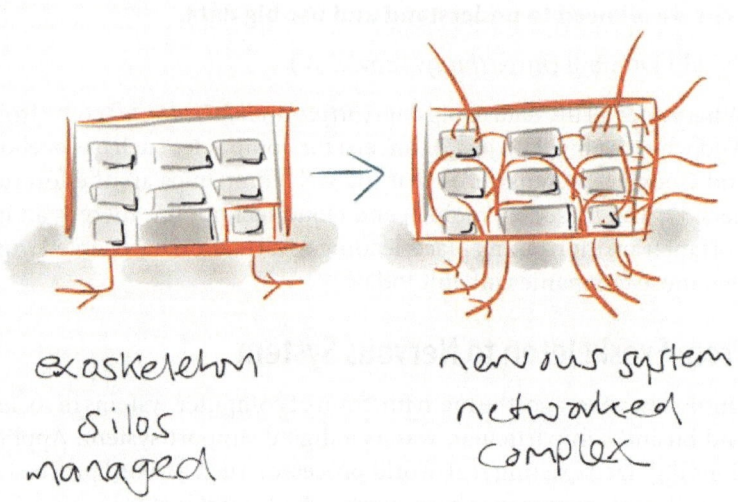

exaskeleton   nervous system
silos   networked
managed   complex

Charting the Transition

As technology has progressed within business, each step taken has resulted in a leap in data volume. To people looking at big data now, a reasonable question is to ask why, when their business isn't Google or Facebook, does big data apply to them?

The answer lies in the ability of web businesses to conduct 100% of their activities online. Their digital nervous system easily stretches from the beginning to the end of their operations. If you have factories, shops, and other parts of the real world within your business, you've further to go in incorporating them into the digital nervous system.

But *further to go* doesn't mean it won't happen. The drive of the Web, social media, mobile, and the cloud is bringing more of each business into a data-driven world. In the UK, the Government Digital Service (*http://bit.ly/1al6EcQ*) is unifying the delivery of services to citizens. The results are a radical improvement of citizen experience, and for the first time many departments are able to get a real picture of how they're doing. For any retailer, companies such as Square (*http://bit.ly/1dpw0QV*), American Express (*http://amex.co/1al6Eto*), and Foursquare (*http://bit.ly/1dpw0Rd*) are bringing payments into a social, responsive data ecosystem, liberating that information from the silos of corporate accounting.

What does it mean to have a digital nervous system? The key trait is to make an organization's feedback loop entirely digital. That is, a direct connection from sensing and monitoring inputs through to product outputs. That's straightforward on the Web. It's getting increasingly easier in retail. Perhaps the biggest shifts in our world will come as sensors and robotics bring the advantages web companies have now to domains such as industry (*http://nyti.ms/1al6FNO*), transport (*http://on.wsj.com/1dpw03w*), and the military (*http://bit.ly/1al6F0m*).

The reach of digital nervous system has grown steadily over the past 30 years, and each step brings gains in agility and flexibility, along with an order of magnitude more data. First, from specific application programs to general business use with the PC. Then, direct interaction over the Web. Mobile adds awareness of time and place, along with instant notification. The next step, to cloud, breaks down data silos and adds storage and compute elasticity through cloud computing. Now, we're integrating smart agents, able to act on our behalf, and connections to the real world through sensors and automation.

Coming, Ready or Not

If you're not contemplating the advantages of taking more of your operation digital, you can bet your competitors are. As Marc Andreessen wrote last year (*http://on.wsj.com/1mbiYMf*), "Software is eating the world." Everything is becoming programmable.

It's this growth of the digital nervous system that makes the techniques and tools of big data relevant to us today. The challenges of massive data flows, and the erosion of hierarchy and boundaries, will lead us to the statistical approaches, systems thinking (*http://bit.ly/1al6G4r*), and machine learning we need to cope with the future we're inventing.

Follow Up on Big Data and Civil Rights

Further reading and discussion on the civil rights implications of big data.

By Alistair Croll (*http://bit.ly/1al6D8J*)

A few weeks ago, I wrote a post about big data and civil rights, which seems to have hit a nerve. It was posted on *Solve for Interesting* (*http://bit.ly/1al6GBi*) and on *Radar* (*http://oreil.ly/1dpw2s1*), and then folks like *Boing Boing* (*http://bit.ly/1al6GBv*) picked it up.

I haven't had this kind of response to a post before (well, I've had responses, such as the comments to this piece for *GigaOm* (*http://bit.ly/1dpw3MM*) five years ago, but they haven't been nearly as thoughtful).

Some of the best posts have really added to the conversation. Here's a list of those I suggest for further reading and discussion.

Nobody Notices Offers They Don't Get

On Oxford's *Practical Ethics* blog (*http://bit.ly/1al6IJD*), Anders Sandberg argues that transparency and reciprocal knowledge about how data is being used will be essential. Anders captured the core of my concerns in a single paragraph, saying what I wanted to far better than I could:

> … nobody notices offers they do not get. And if these absent opportunities start following certain social patterns (for example, not offering them to certain races, genders, or sexual preferences) they can have a deep civil rights effect.

To me, this is a key issue, and it responds eloquently to some of the comments on the original post. Harry Chamberlain commented:

> However, what would you say to the criticism that you are seeing lions in the darkness? In other words, the risk of abuse certainly exists, but until we see a clear case of big data enabling and fueling discrimination, how do we know there is a real threat worth fighting?

I think that this is precisely the point: you can't see the lions in the darkness, because you're not aware of the ways in which you're being disadvantaged. If whites get an offer of 20% off, but minorities don't, that's basically a 20% price hike on minorities—but it's just marketing, so apparently it's okay.

Context Is Everything

Mary Ludloff of Patternbuilders asks, "When does someone else's problem become ours?" Mary is a presenter (*http://oreil.ly/1dpw43e*) at Strata, and an expert on digital privacy. She has a very pragmatic take on things. One point Mary makes is that all this analysis is about prediction—we're taking a ton of data and making a prediction about you:

> The issue with data, particularly personal data, is this: context is everything. And if you are not able to personally question me, you are guessing the context.

If we (mistakenly) predict something, and act on it, we may have wronged someone. Mary makes clear that this is thoughtcrime—arresting someone because their behavior looked like that of a terrorist, or pedophile, or thief. Firing someone because their email patterns suggested they weren't going to make their sales quota. That's the injustice.

This is actually about negative rights (*http://bit.ly/1al6Jgw*), which Wikipedia describes as:

> Rights considered negative rights may include civil and political rights (*http://bit.ly/1dpw3fR*) such as freedom of speech (*http://bit.ly/1al6JwZ*), private property (*http://bit.ly/1dpw4QL*), freedom from violent crime (*http://bit.ly/1al6JNx*), freedom of worship (*http://bit.ly/1dpw57g*), habeas corpus (*http://bit.ly/1al6K48*), a fair trial (*http://bit.ly/1dpw7fq*), freedom from slavery (*http://bit.ly/1al6KkI*).

Most philosophers agree that negative rights outweigh positive ones (i.e., I have a right to fresh air more than you have a right to smoke around me). So our negative right (to be left unaffected by your predictions) outweighs your positive one. As analytics comes closer and closer to predicting actual behavior (*http://dailym.ai/1dpw7vY*), we need to remember the lesson of negative rights.

Big Data Is the New Printing Press

Lori Witzel compares the advent of big data to the creation of the printing press (*http://bit.ly/1al6L8h*), pointing out—somewhat optimistically—that once books were plentiful, it was hard to control the spread of information. She has a good point—we're looking at things from this side of the big data singularity:

> And as the cost of big data and big data analytics drops, I predict we'll see a similar dispersion of technology, and similar destabilizations to societies where these technologies are deployed.

There's a chance that we'll democratize access to information so much that it'll be the corporations, not the consumers, that are forced to change.

While You Slept Last Night

TIBCO's Chris Taylor, standing in for Kashmir Hill at Forbes, paints a dystopian picture of video-as-data (*http://onforb.es/1dpw7Mt*), and just how much tracking we'll face in the future:

> This makes laughable the idea of an implanted chip as the way to monitor a population. We've implanted that chip in our phones, and in video, and in nearly every way we interact with the world. Even paranoids are right sometimes.

I had a wide-ranging chat with Chris last week. We're sure to spend more time on this in the future.

The Veil of Ignorance

The idea for the original post (*http://bit.ly/1al6GBi*) came from a conversation I had with some civil rights activists in Atlanta a few months ago, who hadn't thought about the subject. They (or their parents) walked with Martin Luther King, Jr. But to them big data was "just tech." That bothered me, because unless we think of these issues in the context of society and philosophy, bad things will happen to good people.

Perhaps the best tool for thinking about these ethical issues is the Veil of Ignorance (*http://bit.ly/1dpw8QE*). It's a philosophical exercise for deciding social issues that goes like this:

1. Imagine you don't know where you will be in the society you're creating. You could be a criminal, a monarch, a merchant, a pauper, an invalid.
2. Now design the best society you can.

Simple, right? When we're looking at legislation for big data, this is a good place to start. We should set privacy, transparency, and use policies without knowing whether we're ruling or oppressed, straight or gay, rich or poor.

Three Kinds of Big Data

Looking ahead at big data's role in enterprise business intelligence, civil engineering, and customer relationship optimization.

By Alistair Croll (*http://bit.ly/1al6D8J*)

In the past couple of years, marketers and pundits have spent a lot of time labeling everything *big data*. The reasoning goes something like this:

- Everything is on the Internet.
- The Internet has a lot of data.
- Therefore, everything is big data.

When you have a hammer, everything looks like a nail. When you have a Hadoop deployment, everything looks like big data. And if you're trying to cloak your company in the mantle of a burgeoning industry, big data will do just fine. But seeing big data everywhere is a sure way to hasten the inevitable fall from the peak of high expectations to the trough of disillusionment (*http://bit.ly/1dpw8zU*).

We saw this with cloud computing. From early idealists saying everything would live in a magical, limitless, free data center to today's pragmatism about virtualization and infrastructure, we soon took off our rose-colored glasses and put on welding goggles so we could actually build stuff.

So Where Will Big Data Go To Grow Up?

Once we get over ourselves and start rolling up our sleeves, I think big data will fall into three major buckets: enterprise BI, civil engineering, and customer relationship optimization. This is where we'll see most IT spending, most government oversight, and most early adoption in the next few years.

Enterprise BI 2.0

For decades, analysts have relied on business intelligence (BI) products like Hyperion (*http://bit.ly/1al6Oku*), Microstrategy (*http://bit.ly/1dpw9E8*) and Cognos (*http://ibm.co/1al6MsP*) to crunch large amounts of information and generate reports. Data warehouses and BI tools are great at answering the same question—such as "What were Mary's sales this quarter?"—over and over again. But they've been less good at the exploratory, what-if, unpredictable questions that matter for planning and decision making because that kind of fast exploration of unstructured data is traditionally hard to do and therefore expensive.

Most "legacy" BI tools are constrained in two ways:

- First, they've been schema-then-capture tools in which the analyst decides what to collect, then later captures that data for analysis.
- Second, they've typically focused on reporting what Avinash Kaushik (*http://bit.ly/1iKykdo*) (channeling Donald Rumsfeld) refers to as *known unknowns*—things we know we don't know, and generate reports for.

These tools are used for reporting and operational purposes, and are usually focused on controlling costs, executing against an existing plan, and reporting on how things are going.

As my Strata co-chair Edd Dumbill (*http://bit.ly/1al6MJi*) pointed out when I asked for thoughts on this piece:

> The predominant functional application of big data technologies today is in ETL (extract, transform, and load). I've heard the figure that it's about 80% of Hadoop applications. Just the real grunt work of logfile or sensor processing before loading into an analytic database like Vertica.

The availability of cheap, fast computers and storage, as well as open source tools, have made it okay to capture first and ask questions later. That changes how we use data because it lets analysts speculate beyond the initial question that triggered the collection of data.

What's more, the speed with which we can get results—sometimes as fast as a human can ask them—makes data easier to explore interactively. This combination of interactivity and speculation takes BI into the realm of *unknown unknowns*, the insights that can produce a competitive advantage or an out-of-the-box differentiator.

Cloud computing underwent a transition from promise to compromise. First big, public clouds wooed green-field startups. Then, a few years later, incumbent IT vendors introduced private cloud offerings. These private clouds included only a fraction of the benefits of their public cousins—but were nevertheless a sufficient blend of smoke, mirrors, and features to delay the inevitable move to public resources by a few years and appease the business. For better or worse, that's where most IT cloud budgets are being spent today according to IDC (*http://bit.ly/1dpwarC*), Gartner (*http://gtnr.it/1al6Poi*), and others. Big data adoption will undergo a similar cycle.

In the next few years, then, look for acquisitions and product introductions—and not a little vaporware—as BI vendors that enterprises trust bring them *big data lite*: enough innovation and disruption to satisfy the CEO's golf buddies, but not so much that enterprise IT's jobs are threatened. This, after all, is how change comes to big organizations.

Ultimately, we'll see traditional known unknowns BI reporting living alongside big-data-powered data import and cleanup, and fast, exploratory data unknown unknown interactivity.

Civil Engineering

The second use of big data is in society and government. Already, data mining can be used to predict disease outbreaks, understand traffic patterns, and improve education.

Cities are facing budget crunches, infrastructure problems, and a crowding from rural citizens. Solving these problems is urgent, and cities are perfect labs for big data initiatives. Take a metropolis like New York: hackathons, open feeds of public data, and a population that generates a flood of information as it shops, commutes, gets sick, eats, and just goes about its daily life.

I think municipal data is one of the big three for several reasons: **it's a good tie-breaker for partisanship**, we have **new interfaces everyone can understand**, and we finally have a **mostly connected citizenry**.

In an era of partisan bickering (*http://lat.ms/1dpwaYy*), hard numbers can settle the debate. So they're not just good government; they're good politics. Expect to see big data applied to social issues, helping us to make funding more effective and scarce government resources more efficient (perhaps to the chagrin of some public servants and lobbyists). As this works in the world's biggest cities, it'll spread to smaller ones, to states, and to municipalities.

Making data accessible to citizens is possible, too: Siri and Google Now show the potential for personalized agents; Narrative Science takes complex data and turns it into words the masses can consume easily; Watson and Wolfram Alpha can give smart answers, either through curated reasoning or making smart guesses.

For the first time, we have a connected citizenry armed (for the most part) with smartphones. Nielsen estimated that smartphones would overtake feature phones in 2011 (*http://bit.ly/1al6PEU*), and that concentration is high in urban cores. The App Store is full of apps for bus schedules, commuters, local events, and other tools that can quickly become how governments connect with their citizens and manage their bureaucracies.

The consequence of all this, of course, is more data. Once governments go digital, their interactions with citizens can be easily instrumented and analyzed for waste or efficiency. That's sure to provoke resistance from those who don't like the scrutiny or accountability, but it's a side effect of digitization: every industry that goes digital gets analyzed and optimized, whether it likes it or not.

Customer Relationship Optimization

The final home of applied big data is marketing. More specifically, it's improving the relationship with consumers so companies can, as Sergio Zyman (*http://bit.ly/1dpwd6P*) once said, sell them more stuff, more often, for more money, more efficiently.

The biggest data systems today are focused on web analytics, ad optimization, and the like. Many of today's most popular architectures were weaned on ads and marketing, and have their ancestry in direct marketing plans. They're just more focused than the comparatively blunt instruments (*http://bit.ly/1al6Qsm*) with which direct marketers used to work.

The number of contact points in a company has multiplied significantly. Where once there was a phone number and a mailing address, today there are web pages, social media accounts, and more. Tracking users across all these channels—and turning every click, like, share, friend, or retweet into the start of a long funnel that leads, inexorably, to revenue is a big challenge. It's also one that companies like Salesforce understand, with its investments in chat, social media monitoring, co-browsing, and more.

This is what's lately been referred to as the "360-degree customer view" (though it's not clear that companies will actually act on customer data (*http://oreil.ly/1dpweaY*) if they have it, or whether doing so will become a compliance minefield (*http://oreil.ly/1dpw2s1*)). Big data is already intricately linked to online marketing, but it will branch out in two ways.

First, it'll go from online to offline. Near-field-equipped smartphones with ambient check-in are a marketer's wet dream, and they're coming to pockets everywhere. It'll be possible to track queue lengths, store traffic, and more, giving retailers fresh insights into their brick-and-mortar sales. Ultimately, companies will bring the optimization that online retail has enjoyed to an offline world as consumers become trackable (*http://bit.ly/1dpweHK*).

Second, it'll go from Wall Street (or maybe that's Madison Avenue and Middlefield Road) to Main Street. Tools will get easier to use, and while small businesses might not have a BI platform, they'll have a tablet or a smartphone that they can bring to their places of business. Mobile payment players like Square (*http://bit.ly/1dpw0QV*) are already making them reconsider the checkout process. Adding portable customer intelligence to the tool suite of local companies will broaden how we use marketing tools.

Headlong into the Trough

That's my bet for the next three years, given the molasses of market confusion, vendor promises, and unrealistic expectations we're about to contend with. Will big data change the world? Absolutely. Will it be able to defy the usual cycle of earnest adoption, crushing disappointment, and eventual rebirth all technologies must travel? Certainly not.

Real Data

Big data became *real* in 2013.

If you ask the architects of Obama's re-election campaign, they will tell you that the victory can be directly attributed to the organizers of the ground operation to "get out the vote" on election day. Ask anyone else who watched the operation and the answer will be "big data." While it was clear that Obama For America had an effective wave of volunteers, it was also clear that Harper Reed's gang of technologists was making heavy use of big data to parse user intentions and to engage people through several social media platforms. Obama was re-elected by a smaller margin (4%) in 2012 than his initial election to the Presidency (7%), and many attribute his second victory to his army of technologists and data scientists who made such large-scale use of data that they exceeded the capacity of several Amazon Web Services data centers.

This chapter contains stories that relate to such real-world uses of big data. Journalists such as Alex Howard and Jon Bruner cover topics like Hurricane Sandy, the 2012 presidential election, and the use of big data to monitor activity. Edd Dumbill makes some predictions about big data in 2013 as well, and Julie Steele discusses the potential for big data and 3-D bioprinting.

Finding and Telling Data-Driven Stories in Billions of Tweets

Twitter has hired *Guardian* Data Editor Simon Rogers as its first data editor.

By Alex Howard (*http://bit.ly/1dpweYi*)

Twitter has hired its first data editor. Simon Rogers (*http://bit.ly/1al6RfV*), one of the leading practitioners of data journalism in the world, will join Twitter (*http://bit.ly/1dpwhn5*) in May. He will be moving his family from London to San Francisco and applying his skills to telling data-driven stories using tweets. James Ball (*http://bit.ly/1al6Rg6*) will replace him as *The Guardian*'s new data editor.

As a data editor, will Rogers keep editing and producing something that we'll recognize as journalism? Will his work at Twitter be different than what Google Think (*http://bit.ly/1dpwhDF*) or Facebook Stories (*http://bit.ly/1al6Rwx*) delivers? Different in terms of how he tells stories with data? Or is the difference that Twitter has a lot more revenue coming in or sees data-driven storytelling as core to driving more business? (Rogers wouldn't comment on those counts.)

The gig clearly has potential and Rogers clearly has demonstrable capacity. As he related to me today, in an interview, "What I'm good at is explaining data, simplifying it and making it accessible."

That's a critical set of skills in business, government, or media today. Data-driven journalists have to understand data sources, quality, context, and underlying biases. That's equally true of Twitter. Pew Research reminded us in 2013 that Twitter is not representative of everyone and is often at odds with public opinion (*http://bit.ly/1dpwhUa*).

Tweets aren't always a reliable source to understand everything that happens in the world but it's undeniable that useful insights can be found there. It has become a core component of the set of digital tools and platforms that journalists apply in their work, connected to smartphone phones, pens, water bottles, and notebooks. News frequently breaks on Twitter first and is shared by millions of users independently of any media organization. Journalists now use Twitter to apply a trade that's well over a century old: gather and fact-check reports, add context, and find the truth of what's happening. (Picking up the phone and going to a location still matter, naturally.) The amount of misinformation (*http://bit.ly/1al6RN5*) on Twitter during major news events puts a high premium on the media debunking rumors and sharing accurate facts.

Will the primary difference in Rogers' ability to find truth and meaning in the tweets be access to Twitter's full Firehose, developers, and processing power? His work will have to be judged on its own merits. Until he starts his new gig in May, the following interview offers more insight into why he joined Twitter and how he's thinking about what he'll be doing there.

Why leave the paper now?

Simon Rogers: I love *The Guardian* and have always wanted to work here. I grew up in a house where we read two papers: *The Guardian* during the week and *The Observer* on Sundays. I've had offers but this is the first job where it's become a serious possibility.

There are a few reasons.

Firstly, Twitter is an amazing phenomenon. It's changed every level of how we work as reporters. We really saw that during the "Reading the Riots" project (*http://bit.ly/1dpwir9*). There we had 1.6 million riot-related tweets that Twitter gave us to analyze.

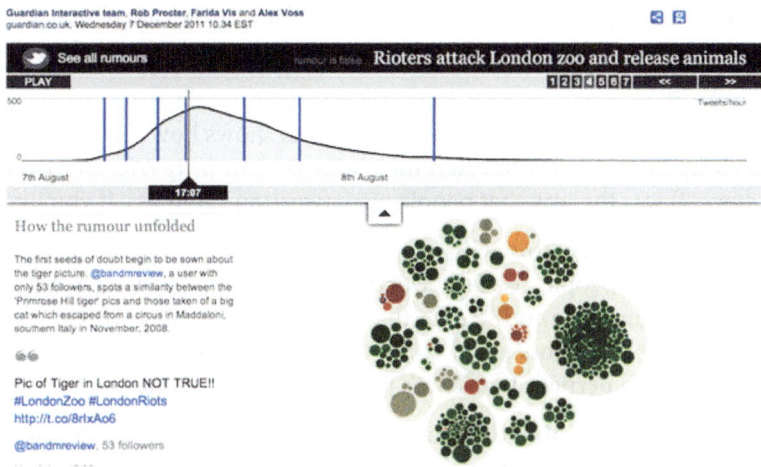

That was important because politicians were agitating about the "role" of Twitter during the disturbances. The work that our team did with academics at Manchester and the subsequent interactive (*http://bit.ly/1al6SjY*) produced by Alastair Dant and the interactive team here opened my eyes to the facts that:

- Twitter and the way it's used tells us a lot about every aspect of life
- The data behind those tweets can really shine a light on the big stories of the moment
- If you can combine that data with brilliant developers you have a really powerful tool

Secondly, Twitter is an amazing place from what I've seen so far. There's a real energy about the place and some brilliant people doing fascinating things. I love the idea of being part of that team.

Thirdly, I've been at *The Guardian* nearly 15 years. I am so comfortable and confident in what I do there that I need a new challenge. This all just came together at the right time.

As a data-driven journalist, you've had to understand data sources, quality, context, and underlying biases. How does that apply to Twitter?

Simon Rogers: Absolutely. Mark Twain said "a lie can be halfway around the world before the truth has got its boots on." All social media encourages that.

I think the work we did with the riot tweets shows how the truth can catch up fast. What interested me about Boston (*http://b.globe.com/1dpwgj2*) was the way that people were tweeting calmness, if you like.

I think we've seen this with the Datablog (*http://bit.ly/1al6SAz*) in general: that people used to worry that the masses weren't clever enough to understand the data that we were publishing. In fact, the community self-rights itself, correcting errors other readers or even ourselves had perpetrated. That's really interesting to me.

What will you be able to do at Twitter with data that you couldn't do at *The Guardian* data desk?

Simon Rogers: Just to be there, in the midst of that data, will be amazing. I think it will make me better at what I do. And I hope I have something to offer them, too.

Will you be using the same tools as you've been applying at *The Guardian*?

Simon Rogers: I'm looking forward to learning some new ones. I'm comfortable with what I know. It's about time I became uncomfortable.

Twitter has some of the world's best data scientists. What makes being a data editor different from being a data scientist?

Simon Rogers: I'm not the world's best statistician. I'm not even very good at maths. I guess what I've been doing at *The Guardian* is acting as a human bridge between data that's tricky to understand and a wider audience that wants to understand it. Isn't that what all data journalism is?

My take on being a data editor at *The Guardian* was that I used it as a way to make data more accessible–crucially, the understanding of it. I need to understand it to make it clear to others, and I want to explain that data in ways that I can understand. Is that the difference between data editors and data scientists? I don't know; I think a lot of these definitions are artificial anyway.

It's like people getting data journalism and data visualization mixed up. I think they are probably different things and involve different processes, but in the end, does it matter anyway?

"Startups Don't Really Know What They Are at the Beginning"

An interview with Alistair Croll and Benjamin Yoskovitz on using lean analytics in a startup

By Ann Spencer (*http://bit.ly/1al6AtD*)

Alistair Croll (*http://bit.ly/1al6D8J*) and Benjamin Yoskovitz (*http://bit.ly/1dpwjeD*) wrote the upcoming book *Lean Analytics: Use Data to Build a Better Startup Faster (http://oreil.ly/VoRrxo)*. In the following interview, they discuss the inspiration behind their book, the unique aspects of using analytics in a startup environment, and more.

What inspired both of you to write your book?

A big part of the inspiration came from our work with Year One Labs (*http://bit.ly/1dpwk26*), an early stage accelerator that we co-founded with two other partners in 2010. We implemented a lean startup program that we put the startups through and provided them with up to 12 months of hands-on mentorship. We saw with these companies as well as others that we've worked on ourselves, advised, and invested in, that they struggled with what to measure, how to measure it, and why to measure certain things.

The core principle of lean startup is build, measure, and learn. While most entrepreneurs understand the *build* part, since they're often technical founders that are excellent at building stuff, they had a hard time with the *measure* and *learn* parts of the cycle. Lean analytics is a way of codifying that further, without being overly prescriptive. We hope it provides a practical and deeper guide to implementing lean startup principles successfully and using analytics to genuinely affect your business.

What are some of the unique aspects to using analytics in a startup environment?

One of the biggest challenges with using analytics in a startup environment is the vast amount of unknowns that a startup faces. Startups don't really know what they are at the beginning. In fact, they shouldn't even be building a product to solve a problem. In many ways they're building products to learn what to build. Learning in an environment of risk and uncertainty is hard. So tracking things is also hard. Startups are also heavily influenced by what they see around them. They see companies that seem to be growing really quickly, the latest hottest trend, competition and so on. Those influences can negatively affect a startup's focus and the rigorous approach needed to find true insight and grow a real business. Lean Analytics is meant to poke a hole in an entrepreneur's reality distortion field, and encourage…or force!…a level of focus and attention that can cut out the noise and help founders move as quickly as possible without doing so blindly.

What defines a good metric?

Good metrics have a few qualities. For starters, a good metric should be a ratio or rate. It makes the number easier to compare. You want to avoid absolute numbers that always go up and to the right. Those are typically vanity metrics.

A good metric has to be incredibly easy to understand. You should be able to tell anyone the number and they can instantly understand what you're doing and why.

A good metric, ultimately, has to change the way you behave. Or at least provide the opportunity for you to change. If you're tracking a number and can't figure out how changes in that number—whether it be up, down, or sideways—would impact how you behave and what you do, then it's a bad number. It probably isn't worth tracking and certainly not worth focusing on. Good metrics are designed to improve decision making.

What are the stages of lean analytics?

We've defined five stages of lean analytics: empathy, stickiness, virality, revenue, and scale. We believe all startups go through these stages in this order, although we've certainly seen exceptions. And we've defined these stages as a way of focusing on a startup's lifecycle and how the metrics change as a startup moves from one stage to the next. We've also created gates through which a startup goes to help it decide whether it's ready to move to the next stage.

Empathy is all about getting out of the building and identifying problems worth solving. It's about key insights that you'll learn from interviewing customers, which guides you to a solution. The metrics you track here are largely qualitative, but you may also start to look at levels of interest you can drive to a website or landing page and early conversion. Basically, you have to answer the question: Does anyone really care about what I'm doing?

Stickiness is about proving that people use your product, which early on is a *minimum viable product*, or MVP, and that people remain engaged. You're going to track the percent of active users, frequency of use, and try to qualitatively understand if you're providing the value you promised to customers.

Virality is about figuring out and growing your acquisition channels. Now that you have a product that's working reasonably well with early adopters, how do you grow the list of users and see if they too become active and engaged? The metric to track here is viral coefficient, which in a perfect world is above 1, meaning that every active user invites one other user that becomes active, in which case you can grow quite quickly…but it's not the only metric that matters. You want to track actions within your application or product that are designed to encourage virality. This might be invites or shares. You have to look at the difference between inherent and artificial virality as well. Ultimately, you get through this stage when you've proven that you can acquire users reasonably well, and you see scalable opportunities to do so going forward.

Revenue is about providing the fundamentals of the business model. Prior to getting to this stage you may have been charging money, but you weren't focused on fine tuning that aspect of the business. And you were properly spending money to acquire customers but not really focusing on whether the economics made sense. Now you have to prove the economics. So you look at things like the *customer lifetime value* and compare that to the *customer acquisition cost*. You might look at the *customer acquisition payback*, which is how long does it take a customer to pay back the acquisition cost you made to bring them in. You're likely going to look at conversion from free to paid, especially if you are building a freemium business. You're also going to look at churn, or how many people abandon your product or service. To get through this stage, you need to have a reasonably well-oiled financial machine that makes sense.

Scale is about growing the business as big as possible. You know you can acquire customers, you know a good enough percentage will stick around and pay, and you know the economics make sense. So now you have to grow. Depending on your business, you'll be looking at different channels such as partners or growing a bigger sales team, APIs for developing an ecosystem, business development opportunities and so on. You may expand into new markets, develop secondary, or ancillary products as well.

The book is filled with case studies. How did both of you decide which case studies to include in the book and why?

It wasn't a complicated process. Many of the case studies came from people we knew and who were leveraging lean startup and analytics in a meaningful way. Some of them came from our own experience. We felt it was important to share those as well. As we developed the framework for the book, such as tackling different business models, the Lean Analytics stages, etc., we looked for great examples that could speak to each of the key points we were making. We talk a great deal in the book about *the one metric that matters*. This basically means: focus on one metric only, at any given time. This came from our experience but also from talking to a lot of other people. Then we picked a couple of great stories or case studies that reflected the importance of the concept.

It was important for us to have real-world examples of all types of companies, whether they were big, small, successful, less so, early stage, late stage, etc., so there would be variety, but also because we know these examples resonate a great deal with people. We know that people are looking for proof that lean works and that a focus on analytics matters; hopefully we've been able to provide that in the book (*http:// oreil.ly/VoRrxo*).

On the Power and Perils of "Preemptive Government"

Stephen Goldsmith on the potential of urban predictive data analytics in municipal government.

By Alex Howard (*http://bit.ly/1dpweYi*)

The last time I spoke with Stephen Goldsmith, he was the deputy mayor of New York City, advocating for increased use of *citizensourcing* (*http://oreil.ly/1al6YIz*), where government uses technology tools to tap into the distributed intelligence of residents to understand—and fix—issues around its streets, on its services, and even within institutions. In the years since, as a professor at the Ash Center for Democratic Governance and Innovation at the John F. Kennedy School of Government at Harvard University, the former mayor of Indianapolis has advanced the notion of *preemptive government* (*http://bit.ly/1dpwkPF*).

That focus caught my attention, given that my colleague, Alistair Croll (*http://bit.ly/1al6D8J*), had published several posts on Radar looking at the ethics around big data (*http://bit.ly/1dpwl6n*). The increasing use of data mining and algorithms by government to make decisions based upon pattern recognition and assumptions regarding future actions is a trend worth watching. Will guaranteeing government data quality become mission critical, once high profile mistakes are made? Any assessment of the perils and promise of a data-driven society (*http://nyti.ms/1al6WQP*) will have to include a reasoned examination of the growing power of these applied algorithms to the markets and the lives of our fellow citizens.

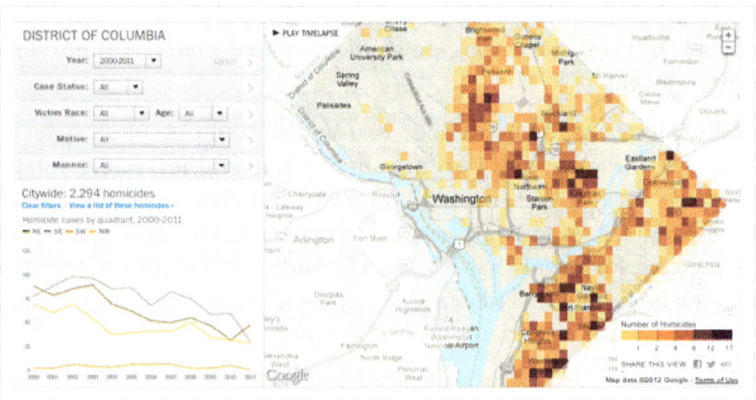

Given some of those concerns, I called Goldsmith up this winter to learn more about what he meant.

Our interview, lightly edited for content and clarity, follows.

When you say "preemptive government," what do you mean?

Stephen Goldsmith: I'm thinking about the intersection of trends here. One is what we might talk about as big data and data analytics. Inside, government has massive amounts of information located in all sorts of different places that if one looked at analytically, we could figure out which restaurants are most likely to have problems, which contractors are most likely to build bad buildings and the like.

For the first time, through the combination of digital processes, mobile tools, and big data analytics, government can make preemptive solutions. Government generally responds to problems and then measures its performance by the number of activities it conducts, as contrasted to the problems it solves. New York City and Chicago have begun to take the lead in this area in specific places. When I was in New York City, we were trying to figure out how to set up a data analytics center. New York has started (*http://bit.ly/1dpwlDc*) to do some of that, so that we can predict where the next event's going to occur and then solve it. That eventually needs to be merged with community sentiment mining, but it's a slightly different issue.

What substantive examples exist of this kind of approach making a difference?

Stephen Goldsmith: We are now operating a mayoral performance analytics initiative (*http://bit.ly/1al6ZMo*) at the Kennedy School, trying to create energy around the solutions. We are featuring people who are doing it well, bringing folks together.

New York City, through a fellow named Mike Flowers (*http://bit.ly/1dpwlDc*), has begun to solve specific problems in building violations and restaurant inspections. He's overcoming the obstacles where all of the legacy CIOs say they can't share data. He's showing that you can.

Chicago (*http://oreil.ly/1al6XnL*) is just doing remarkable stuff in a range of areas, from land use planning to crime control, like deciding how to intervene earlier in solving crimes.

Indiana has begun working on child welfare using analytics to figure out best outcomes for children in tough circumstances. They're using analytics to measure which providers are best for which young adults that are in trouble, what type of kid is most successful with what type of mental health treatment, drug treatment, mentoring, or the like.

I think these are all just scratching the surface. They need to be highlighted so that city and state leaders can understand how they can have dramatically better returns on their investments by identifying these issues in advance.

Who else is sharing and consuming data to do predictive data analytics in the way that you're describing?

Stephen Goldsmith: A lot of well-known staff programs, like ComStat or CityStat, do a really good job of measuring activities. When combined with analytics, they'll be able to move into managing outcomes more effectively. There are a lot of folks, like in San Francisco, beginning to look at these issues, but I think New York City and Chicago are really in the lead.

Based upon their example, what kinds of budget, staffing, and policy decisions would other cities need to make to realize similar returns?

Stephen Goldsmith: The most restrictive element in government today is the no-longer-accurate impression that legacy data can't be easily integrated. Every agency has a CIO who often believes it's his or her job to protect that data. I'm not talking about privacy; I'm just talking about data integrity. We know that there's a range of tools that will allow relatively easy integration and data mining.

Another lesson is that this really needs to be driven by the mayor or the governor. The answers to problems come from picking up data across agencies, not just managing the data inside your agency. Without city hall or gubernatorial leadership, it's very difficult to drive data analytics.

What about the risks of preemptive government leading to false positives or worse?

Stephen Goldsmith: There is a risk, but let me talk about it in the following way: government can no longer afford to operate the way it operates. You cannot afford to regulate every business as if it's equally bad or equally good. Every restaurant is not equally good or equally bad. Every contractor's not bad or good. There are bad guys and good guys, and good performers and bad performers. There are families that need help and families that don't need help. We need to allocate our resources most effectively to create solutions. That means we need to look at which solutions work for which problems.

What do we know about which contractors have a history of being bad? I don't mean "bad" like just how they build: I mean have they paid their taxes right, do they discriminate in the marketplace; whatever those factors are in order to target our resources.

That means that when Flowers did this in New York, we got several hundred buildings that were the most likely to burn down. We knew that from analytics. We're going to go out and mitigate those buildings. Could we make a mistake and say that 10 of those 300 buildings really aren't that bad? Absolutely, but it's a much better targeting of resources and it's the only way government can afford to effectively operate.

There are other issues, too, like personalization, where we have a lot of privacy issues, and "opt in" and "opt out" where people may want a personal relationship with their government. That's a little different than predictive analytics, but it raises privacy issues.

Then we have a fascinating question, one that social work communities and criminal justice communities worry about, which is, "Okay, you can predict the likelihood that somebody can be hurt, or that somebody will commit a crime, and adjust resources accordingly—but we better be pretty careful because it raises a lot of ethics questions and profiling questions."

My short answer is that these are important, legitimate questions. We can't ignore them, but if we continue to do business the way we do it has more negative trade-offs than not.

Speaking of personalization and privacy, has mining social media for situational awareness during national disasters or other times of crisis become a part of the toolkit for cities?

Stephen Goldsmith: The conversation we've had has been about how to use enterprise data to make better decisions, right? That's basically going to open up a lot of insight, but that model is pretty arrogant. It basically ignores crowd sourcing. It assumes that really smart people in government with a lot of data will make better solutions. But we know that people in communities can co-produce information together. They can crowdsource solutions.

In New York City, we actually had some experience with this. One thread was the work that Rachel [Haot] was doing to communicate, but we were also using social media on the operations side. I think we're barely getting started on how to mine community sentiment, how to integrate that with 311 data for better solutions, how to prioritize information where people have problems, and how to anticipate the problems early.

You may know that Indianapolis, in the 2012 Super Bowl, had a group of college students and a couple of local providers looking at Twitter conversations in order to intervene earlier. They were geotagged by name and curated to figure out where there was a crime problem, where somebody needed parking, where they were looking for tickets, and where there's too much trash on the ground. It didn't require them to call government. Government was watching the conversation, participating in it and solving the problem.

I think that where we are has lots of potential and is a little bit immature. The work now is to incorporate the community sentiment into the analytics and the mobile tools.

How the World Communicates in 2013

Sneak Peek at Upcoming Session at Strata Santa Clara 2013

By Robert Munro (*http://oreil.ly/1dpwoPB*)

Plain text is the world's largest source of digital information. As the amount of unstructured text grows, so does the percentage of text that is not in English. The *majority* of the world's data is now unstructured text outside of English. So unless you're an exceptional polyglot, you can't understand most of what's out there, even if you want to.

Language technologies underlie many of our daily activities. Search engines, spam filtering, and news personalization (including your social media feeds) all employ smart, adaptive knowledge of how we communicate. We can automate many of these tasks well, but there are places where we fall short. For example, the world's most spoken language, Mandarin Chinese, is typically written without spaces. "解放大道" can mean "Liberation Avenue" or "Solution Enlarged Road" depending on where you interpret the gaps. It's a kind of ambiguity that we only need to worry about in English when we're registering domain names and inventing hashtags (something the folk at "Who Represents" (*http://bit.ly/1al6Xo1*) didn't worry about enough). For Chinese, we still don't get it right with automated systems: the best systems get an error every 20 words or so. We face similar problems for about a quarter of the world's data. We can't even reliably tell you what the words are, let alone extract complex information at scale.

We'll talk more about the state of the art in language technologies at Strata 2013 (*http://oreil.ly/1dpwoPB*). For this article, we decided to answer a more basic question: "How are people actually communicating right now?"

The infographic shows the breakdown of what languages people are using for face-to-face communication, relative to phone-based communication and Internet-enabled communication. By word count, almost 7% of the world's communications are now mediated by digital technologies:

- Every three months, the world's text messages exceed the word count of every book ever published.

- Text is cheap: every utterance since the start of humanity would take up less than 1% of the world's current digital storage capacity (about 50 exabytes, assuming 110 billion people have averaged 16,000 words a day for 20 years each).
- The Twitter Firehose outside the processing capacity of most organizations, would be about the size of dot above the i in English.
- There are more than 6,000 other languages: only the top 1% are shown.
- Not one language from the Americas or Australia made the cut.
- Also omitted, email spam would be larger than every block except spoken Mandarin (官話).
- Short messages (SMS and instant messaging) account for nearly 2% of the world's communications. This makes short message communication the most popular and linguistically diverse form of written communication that has ever existed.
- If the Facebook 'like' was considered a one-word language, it would be in the top 5% most widely spoken languages (although still outside the top 200).
- Your browser probably won't show Sundanese script (ᮞᮥᮔ᮪ ᮓ ᮞ), even though the world's Sundanese speakers outnumber the populations of New York, London, Tokyo, and Moscow, combined.
- You misread that last point as "Sudanese," which is a variety of Arabic (العربية) and were surprised at the difference: we have a blind-spot when it comes to knowing about the existence of languages.
- Is a picture worth a 1,000 words? If so, shared pictures would double the size of the social networks block.
- Across all the world's communications, 5 in every 10,000 words are directed at machines, not people: mainly search engines.

Perhaps the most surprising outcome for many people will be the relatively small footprint of Internet publications (www). Between all the news sites, blogs, and other sites, we simply aren't adding that much content when counting by words produced. The persistence of web pages means that they are consumed more often, and there is a bias towards more dominant languages like English, especially in areas like technology and scientific publications. But when we use digital technologies to communicate, most of us are privately interacting via SMS, email, and instant messaging, and more likely to communicate in our first languages as a result.

As the connected world gradually takes in more of the actual world, we can expect the diversity of technology-enabled communication to more closely align with face-to-face communication. Understanding human communication at scale will be central to the next generation of people-centric technologies.

Big Data Comes to the Big Screen

Using data science to predict the Oscars

By Michael Gold (*http://oreil.ly/1al6XUO*)

Sophisticated algorithms are not going to write the perfect script or crawl YouTube to find the next Justin Bieber (that last one I think we can all be thankful for!). But a model can predict the probability of a nominee winning the Oscar, and recently our model has *Argo* overtaking *Lincoln* as the likely winner of Best Picture. Every day on FarsiteForecast.com (*http://bit.ly/1dpwruK*), we've been describing applications of data science for the media and entertainment industry, illustrating how our models work, and updating the likely winners based on the outcomes of the awards season leading up to the Oscars.

Just as predictive analytics provides valuable decision-making tools in sectors from retail to health care to advocacy, data science can also empower smarter decisions for entertainment executives, which led us to launch the Oscar forecasting project. While the potential for data science to impact any organization is as unique as each company itself, we thought we'd offer a few use cases that have wide application for media and entertainment organizations:

Sales projections
> Everyone wants to know as early as possible how an intellectual property will perform. Predictive analytics can inform box office projections, TV ratings, song downloads, or ticket sales.

Geospatial analysis
> Part of better revenue planning is understanding who and where audiences can be found. Geospatial analysis answers tactical questions on a local level, which drive better analysis and projections.

This includes identifying in which markets and theaters a film will perform best, or which cities a band should hit on a tour.

Marketing optimization

From a film's P&A spend to allocating digital spend on an album release, marketing attribution and micro-targeting optimizes spending and maximizes ROI.

And of course—predicting award winners!

So how do our Oscar forecasting models work? We took decades of movie and Academy Awards data and built regression-based models that isolate the key variables that likely lead to an Oscar win. We combined that historical perspective with real-time data, including betting markets and nominee wins at awards such as Golden Globes leading up to this year's Oscars. The combination of rich historical data and real-time information produces models that aim to capture the long history of Academy voting behavior and the dynamism of nominees generating momentum throughout the awards season.

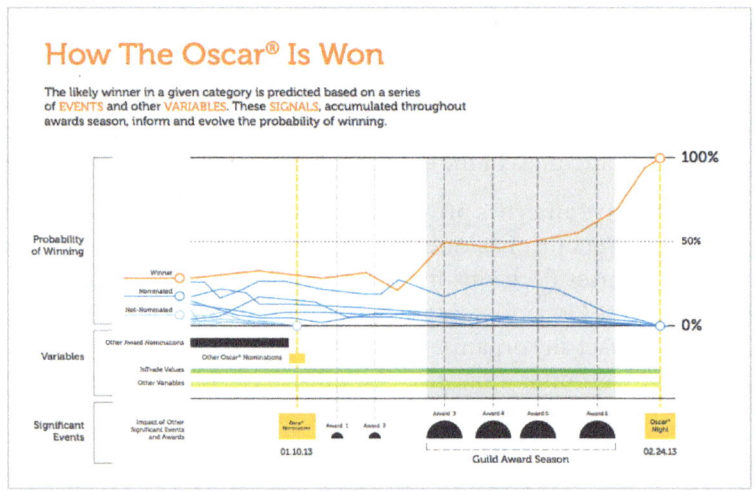

While we are predicting six awards (Best Picture, Best Director, Best Actor, Best Actress, Best Supporting Actor, and Best Supporting Actress), Best Picture garners the most attention. There are a number of key drivers in our model, including a director's previous nominations and wins, odds in the betting markets, wins in the awards season leading up to the Oscars, and total nominations for the film in the current year. This year the total nominations variable favors Spielberg (*Lincoln*), which leads the pack with 12 nominations.

One of the strongest correlations is between Best Picture and Best Director. Directors are rarely nominated without having their film in the Best Picture category. Since 1970, 83.3% of Best Picture winners also won Best Director. Yet there have been significant changes to the nomination process, requiring additional analysis. The Best Picture field is now up to 10 films, while the Best Director category is still 5 nominees. Does this mean that a Best Director nominee is more likely to have their film up for Best Picture and thus the variable should be more important? Or is it less likely that a Best Picture nominee will have its director nominated for Best Director and the strength of variable should be reconsidered?

How a data scientist interprets this analysis significantly informs the outcome of the Best Picture and Best Director models. This question is particularly relevant this year since Ben Affleck and *Argo* have been racking up wins for Director and Film throughout the awards season, even though Affleck is not nominated for the Best Director Oscar. This underscores the importance of the human element of data science. It is crucial for data scientists to understand industry dynamics and build models that are responsive to changes in a fast moving and competitive landscape.

At the end of the day, data science and predictive analytics are incredible tools, which can enhance any executive's decision-making process. The creative geniuses who have built the media industry will further grow and enhance their sector and advance their craft with the insights offered by better data on consumers, the market, and trends. Data science won't replace development executives, media buyers, marketing departments, or studio or network executives. But it will make everyone in the media industry smarter and more informed.

Disclaimer: Oscar,® Oscars,® Oscar Night,® ©A.M.P.A.S.®, and Academy Award(s)® are trademarked by the Academy of Motion Picture Arts and Sciences.

The Business Singularity

How the inevitable rise of software means cycle time trumps scale.

By Alistair Croll (*http://bit.ly/1al6D8J*)

Exponential curves gradually, inexorably grow until they reach a limit. The function increases over time. That's why a force like gravity, which grows exponentially as objects with mass get closer to one another, eventually leads to a black hole. And at the middle of this black hole is a point of infinite mass, a singularity, within which the rules no longer apply.

Financiers also like exponents. "Compound interest is the most powerful force in the universe" is a quote often attributed to Einstein; whoever said it was right. If you pump the proceeds of interest back into a bank account, it'll increase steadily.

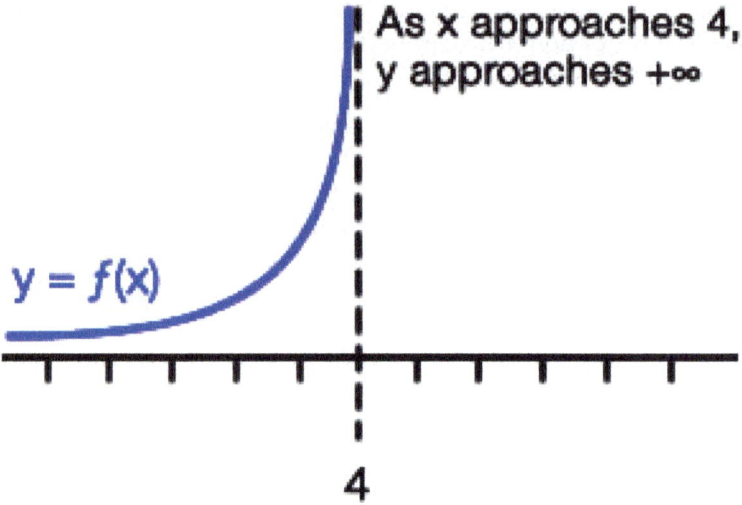

Computer scientists like to throw the term *singularity* around, too. To them, it's the moment when (*http://bit.ly/1dpws1H*) machines *become intelligent enough to make a better machine*. It's the Geek Rapture, the capital-S Singularity. It's the day when machines don't need us any more, and to them, we look like little more than ants. Ray Kurzweil (*http://bit.ly/1al716Y*) thinks it's right around the corner (*http://amzn.to/1dpwsii*)—circa 2045—and after that time, to us, these artificial intelligences will be incomprehensible.

Businesses need to understand singularities, because they have one of their own to contend with.

Business Has Been About Scale

For centuries—since at least the start of the industrial era—business has been about scale. As a business student, I was constantly told that bigger companies have the upper hand. Economies of scale are the only long-term sustainable advantage, because with scale you can control markets, set prices, own channels, influence regulators, and so on.

The embodiment of this obsession with scale is the corporation. You may have issues with today's companies-are-people-too mindset, but remember that they were initially conceived to allow huge projects like transcontinental railroads to happen while shielding the investors from the equally huge risks. Before corporations, it took a monarch to build something truly epic.

The corporation wouldn't be possible without an organization that could itself scale. Daniel McCallum (*http://bit.ly/1al71nv*) first realized that organizational charts and spans of control let the railroads scale (*http://bit.ly/1dpwsyQ*), and we haven't looked back. Just as standardization made the mass production of everything from cars to armaments possible, so the organizational chart made global companies possible.

Scale is so entrenched in our society that it's built into our fundamental economic indicators. Gross domestic product (GDP) rewards national productivity rather than, say, individual productivity or citizen happiness. Can't make your GDP grow by improving things? *Grow your population.*

Thanks to software and big data, however, scale's importance is waning.

Why Software Changes Businesses

Marc Andreessen (*http://bit.ly/1al74jk*) once observed that software is eating the world (*http://on.wsj.com/1dpwqXH*). Once a process becomes digital at one end, and digital at the other, it quickly turns digital in the middle. As the inputs and outputs of industry become increasingly digital, the middle—the organization—becomes software.

Software has two important attributes that fundamentally change how businesses are run.

First, **software can be analyzed**. Digital systems leave a digital exhaust, an analytical breadcrumb trail that happens automatically. An employee doesn't record how long it takes them to do something; *software has no choice but to do so.*

Second, **software can be optimized**. Managing humans is messy. It is fraught with emotion and governed by employment law. But nobody cares about pitting two algorithms against one another in a battle to the death. HR is rough and toothless; software optimization is tough and ruthless. Humans retire; code gets a faster processor.

Analysis and optimization lead to a closed loop of continuous improvement. They give us the exponential function.

Heartless? Maybe. If Hollywood has taught us anything, it's that singularities aren't good for those left behind, as *The Terminator* (*http://bit.ly/1al71Uy*) and *The Matrix* (*http://bit.ly/1dpwu9J*) suggest. Closer to home, one look at the runaway risk of algorithmic trading or the creepy dystopia of wiretapping proves that we haven't yet figured out how to harness our connected world for the greater good.

But remember that the Terminator was a cyborg—literally, a cybernetic organism. Cybernetics is the study of feedback loops. According to Wikipedia (*http://bit.ly/1al72b2*):

> Cybernetics is applicable when a system being analyzed is involved in a closed signaling loop; that is, where action by the system generates some change in its environment and that change is reflected in that system in some manner (feedback) that triggers a system change, originally referred to as a "circular causal" relationship.

The business singularity is about creating a business that analyzes changes in its environments and turns them into system updates. The smartest companies know this. They instrument every facet of their business, and figure out how to tweak it. I joked the other day that Google's business plan is really to get to the singularity first, because after that it won't matter. Maybe that's more right than it seems. Maybe organizations that get to the business singularity first won't care about their competitors.

It's the Cycle, Stupid

Companies that learn to harness the power of data iteratively stop worrying about scale, and start worrying about cycle time. To them, everything is an experiment, a chance to optimize. They analyze everything, and feed this back into themselves, continuously engineering their improved successor. Scale might happen—in fact, it probably does, because software is easy to replicate—but it's a natural consequence of circular, causal loops.

It's this cycle of learning and optimization, accelerated by software and the data exhaust of a connected society, that pushes businesses toward a limit, a point at which they stop behaving like *organizations* and start behaving like *organisms*. Importantly, companies on that side of the business singularity will seem opaque to us, shifting and transient, unthinkably agile. To them, we'll seem sluggish, predictable, and unwise. Like ants.

Figure 3-1. Photo by Tim (dctim1) on Flickr (http://bit.ly/1dpwuqo). Used under a creative commons license. Thanks, Tim!

This seems a bit fanciful, and smarter folks than I (*http://oreil.ly/ 1al756S*) have called it mere hyperbole. So let me offer an example by way of virality.

To an analytics wonk (*http://bit.ly/1dpwtTl*), the number of people who adopt a product because an existing user told them to is measured with the *viral coefficient*. If every user invites at least one other user, you have a business that grows by itself. Hotmail rode virality to a $300 million exit because every email it sent carried an invitation, a natural vector for infection.

But there's a second viral metric that's much less talked about, and sometimes more important: *viral cycle time*. This is the delay between when you sign up, and when someone else does because you told them to.

Back in the early days of YouTube (*http://bit.ly/1al72rR*), there were several video sites competing in the rapidly growing online-video sector. YouTube wasn't the best (*http://bit.ly/1dpwuXs*). It didn't even have the best viral coefficient; companies like Tabblo were doing better. But what YouTube *did* have was really, really good cycle time. People tended to share a video with others more quickly on YouTube than on competing sites. As a result, YouTube quickly left the others in the dust.

Companies like Google (*http://bit.ly/1al72Ig*) and Amazon (*http://bit.ly/1dpwxlU*) care as much about the *cycle time* at which they learn as they do about their ability to generate products and services. Scale is a consequence of iteration or a side effect of replacing things with software. Everything these companies do is an experiment. Scale is OK because it gives them more test subjects and increases the confidence level of their results. But scale isn't the point: quick learning is. As my *Lean Analytics (http://oreil.ly/VoRrxo)* co-author Ben Yoskovitz (*http://bit.ly/1dpwvKR*) says of startups, *the goal is to learn*. They get better, more efficient, and the next cycle is infinitesimally tighter. The curve bends, inexorably and imperceptibly; they approach the limit.

Peculiar Businesses

There's another definition of singularity: *a peculiarity or odd trait*. Today, companies that are passing through to the other side of the business singularity look weird to us. They invest in solar cells (*http://cnet.co/1al76b4*) and goggles (*http://bit.ly/1dpwxTb*). They offer their own infrastructure to competitors, or open source it. They behave strangely (to us, anyway), trading profit for iteration (*http://tcrn.ch/1al76HU*). They get uncomfortably close to customers and critics.

Figure 3-2. Google's investment in Recurrent Energy: large-scale solar PV projects in California

I don't think accountants have a metric for "how fast the organism learns," but they'd better get one soon. For modern businesses—built with little capital expenditures (capex) thanks to clouds, marketed with little investment thanks to social media—learning is a company's greatest asset. Learning faster is enough to unseat titans of industry. Those on the other side of the business singularity live by cycle time; those on this side seldom think about it.

I've definitely abused the notion of a singularity here. Maybe this isn't as tectonic a shift as the rise of sentient machines or the middle of a black hole. But it's more than just the evolution of businesses, because it's the migration from a physical world to a digital one. We're moving from a business ecosystem where those who have scale win, to one where those who have better cycles of adaptation and learning win.

The cycles themselves are driven by data and software. It's something I'm hoping to explore in detail during the Data Driven Business Day at Strata Santa Clara (*http://oreil.ly/1dpwypW*) in late February.

Stacks Get Hacked: The Inevitable Rise of Data Warfare

The cycle of good, bad, and stable has happened at every layer of the stack. It will happen with big data, too.

By Alistair Croll (*http://bit.ly/1al6D8J*)

First, technology is good. Then it gets bad. Then it gets stable.

This has been going on for a long time, likely since the invention of fire, knives, or the printed word. But I want to focus specifically on computing technology. The human race is busy colonizing a second online world and sticking prosthetic brains—today, we call them smartphones—in front of our eyes and ears. And stacks of technology on which they rely are vulnerable.

When we first created automatic phone switches, hackers quickly learned how to blow a Cap'n Crunch whistle to get free calls from pay phones. When consumers got modems, attackers soon figured out how to rapidly redial to get more than their fair share of time on a BBS, or to program scripts that could brute force their way into others' accounts. Eventually, we got better passwords and we fixed the pay phones and switches.

We moved up the networking stack, above the physical and link layers. We tasted TCP/IP, and found it good. Millions of us installed Trumpet Winsock on consumer machines. We were idealists rushing onto the wild open web and proclaiming it a new utopia. Then, because of the way the TCP handshake worked, hackers figured out how to DDOS people with things like SYN attacks. Escalation, and router hardening, ensued.

We built HTTP, and SQL, and more. At first, they were open, innocent, and helped us make huge advances in programming. Then attackers found ways to exploit their weaknesses with cross-site scripting and buffer overruns. They hacked armies of machines to do their bidding, flooding target networks and taking sites offline. Technologies like MP3s gave us an explosion in music, new business models, and abundant crowdsourced audiobooks—even as they leveled a music industry with fresh forms of piracy for which we hadn't even invented laws.

Here's a more specific example of unintended consequences. Paul Mockapetris (*http://bit.ly/1dpwwyx*) is one of the creators of today's Internet. He created DNS and implemented SMTP, fundamental technologies on which all of us rely. But he's also single-handedly responsible for all the spam in the world.

That might be a bit of an overstatement, though I tease him about it from time to time. But there's a nugget of truth to it: DNS was a simplified version of more robust directories like those in X.25. Paul didn't need all that overhead, because he was just trying to solve the problem of remembering all those Internet addresses by hand, not trying to create a hardened, authenticated, resilient address protocol. He also created SMTP, the simple mail transport protocol. It was a whittled down version of MTP—hence the "S"—and it didn't include end-to-end authentication.

These two things—SMTP and DNS—make spam possible. If either of them had some kind of end-to-end authentication, it would be far harder for spammers to send unwanted messages and get away with it. Today, they're so entrenched that attempts to revise email protocols in order to add authentication have consistently failed. We're willing to live with the glut of spam that clogs our servers because of the tremendous value of email.

We owe much of the Internet's growth to simplicity and openness. Because of how Paul built DNS and SMTP, there's no need to go through a complex bureaucracy to start something, or to jump through technical hoops to send an email to someone you met at a bar. We can invite a friend to a new application without strictures and approvals. The Internet has flourished precisely because it was built on a foundation of loose consensus and working code. It's also flourished in spite of it.

Each of these protocols, from the lowly physical connections and links of Ethernet and PPP all the way up through TCP sessions and HTTP transactions, are arranged in a stack, independent layers of a delicious networking cake. By dividing the way the Internet works into discrete layers, innovation can happen at one layer (copper to fiber; token ring to Ethernet; UDP to TCP; Flash to DHTML; and so on) independent of the other layers. We didn't need to rewrite the Internet to build YouTube.

Paul, and the other framers of the Web, didn't know we'd use it to navigate, or stream music—but they left it open so we could. But where the implications of BBS hacking or phone phreaking were limited to a small number of homebrew hackers, the implications for the Web were far bigger, because by now, everyone relied on it.

Anyway, on to big data.

Geeks often talk about "layer 8." When an IT operator sighs resignedly that it's a layer 8 problem, she means it's a human's fault. It's where humanity's rubber meets technology's road. And big data is interesting precisely *because* it's the layer 8 protocol. It's got great power, demands great responsibility, and portends great risk unless we do it right. And just like the layers beneath it, it's going to get good, then bad, then stable.

Other layers of the protocol stack have come under assault by spammers, hackers, and activists. There's no reason to think layer 8 won't as well. And just as hackers find a clever exploit to intercept and spike an SSL session, or trick an app server into running arbitrary code, so they'll find an exploit for big data.

The term *data warfare* might seem a bit hyperbolic, so I'll try to provide a few concrete examples. I'm hoping for plenty more in the Strata Online Conference (*http://bit.ly/1al76Yz*) we're running next week, which has a stellar lineup of people who have spent time thinking about how to do naughty things with information at scale.

Injecting Noise

Analytics applications rely on tags embedded in URLs to understand the nature of traffic they receive. URLs contain parameters that identify the campaign, the medium, and other information on the source of visitors. For example, the URL *http://www.solveforinteresting.com? utm_campaign=datawar* tells Google Analytics to assign visits from that link to the campaign "datawar." There's seldom any verification of this information—with many analytics packages it's included in plain text. Let's say, as a joke, you decide you'd like your name to be the most prolific traffic source on a friend's blog. All you need is a few willing participants, and you can simply visit the blog from many browsers and machines using your name as the campaign tag. You'll be the top campaign traffic source.

This seems innocent enough, until you realize that you can take a similar approach to misleading your competitor. You can make them think a less-effective campaign is outperforming a successful one. You can trick them into thinking Twitter is a better medium than Google +, when in fact the reverse is true, which causes them to pay for customer acquisition in less-effective channels.

The reality isn't this simple—smart businesses track campaigns by outcomes such as purchases rather than by raw visitors. But the point is clear: open-ended data schemes like tagging work because they're extensible and simple, but that also makes them vulnerable. The practice of *googlebombing (http://on.mash.to/1al79DJ)* is a good example. Linking a word or definition to a particular target (such as sending searches for "miserable failure" to a biography on the White House website) simply exploits the openness of Google's underlying algorithms.

But even if you think you have a reliable data source, you may be wrong. Consider that a few years ago, only 324 Athenians reported having swimming pools on their tax returns. This seemed low to some civil servants in Greece, so they decided to check. Using Google Maps, they counted 16,974 of them (*http://nyti.ms/1dpwC9c*)—despite efforts by citizens to camouflage their pools (*http://bit.ly/1al77M0*) under green tarpaulins.

Whether the data is injected, or simply collected unreliably, data's first weakness is its source. Collection is seldom authenticated. There's a reason prosecutors insist on chain of evidence; but big data and analytics, like DNS and SMTP, is usually built for simplicity and ubiquity rather than for resiliency or auditability.

Mistraining the Algorithms

Most of us get attacks almost daily, in the form of spam and phishing. Most of these attacks are blocked by heuristics and algorithms.

Spammers are in a constant arms race with these algorithms. Each message that's flagged as spam is an input into anti-spam algorithms —so if a word like "Viagra" appears in a message you consider spam, then the algorithm is slightly more likely to consider that word "spammy" in future.

If you run a blog, you probably see plenty of comment spam filled with nonsense words—these are attempts to mistrain the machine-learning algorithms that block spammy content by teaching it innocuous words, undermining its effectiveness. You're actually watching a fight between spammers and blockers, played out comment by comment, on millions of websites around the world.

Making Other Attacks More Effective

Anti-spam heuristics happen behind the scenes, and they work pretty well. Despite this, some spam does get through. But when it does, we seldom click on it, because it's easy to spot. It's poorly worded; it comes from an unfamiliar source; it doesn't render properly in our mail client.

What If that Weren't the Case?

A motivated attacker can target an individual. If they're willing to invest time researching their target, they can gain trust or impersonate a friend. The discovery of several nation-state-level viruses aimed at governments and rich targets shows a concerted, handcrafted phishing attack can work. In the hands of an attacker, tools like Facebook's Graph Search or Peekyou are a treasure trove of facts that can be used to craft a targeted attack.

The reason spam is still easy to spot is that it's traditionally been hard to automate this work. People don't dig through your trash unless you're under investigation.

Today, however, consumers have access to big data tools that spy agencies could only dream of a few short years ago. Which means attackers do too, and the effectiveness of phishing, identity theft, and other information crimes will soar once bad actors learn how to harness these tools.

But digging through virtual trash and data exhaust is what machines do best. Big data lets personal attacks work at scale. If smart data scientists with decent grammar tried to maximize spam effectiveness, we'd lose quickly. To them, phishing is just another optimization problem.

Trolling to Polarize

Data warfare doesn't have to be as obvious as injecting falsehoods, mistraining machine-learning algorithms, or leveraging abundant personal data to trick people. It can be far more subtle. Let's say, for example, you wanted to polarize a political discussion such as gun control in order to reduce the reasoned discourse of compromise and justify your hard-lined stance. *All you need to do is get angry.*

A recent study (*http://bit.ly/1dpwC9s*) showed that the tone of comments in a blog post had a tangible impact on how readers responded to the post. When comments used reasonable language, readers' views were more moderate. But when those comments were aggressive, readers hardened their positions. Those that agreed with the post did so more strongly, and those who disagreed objected more fiercely. The chance for compromise vanished.

Similar approaches can sway sentiment-analysis tools that try to gauge public opinion on social platforms. Once reported, these sentiments often form actual opinion, because humans like to side with the majority. Data becomes reality. There are plenty of other examples of *adversarial* data escalation. Consider the programmer who created 800,000 books and injected them into Amazon's catalog (*http://bit.ly/1al7aaJ*). Thanks to the frictionless nature of ebooks and the ease of generating them, he's saturated their catalog (hat tip to Edd (*http://bit.ly/1dpvX7W*) for this one).

The Year of Data Warfare

Data warfare is real. In some cases, such as spam, it's been around for decades. In other cases, like tampering with a competitor's data, it's been possible but too expensive until cloud computing and new algorithms made it cheap and easy. And in many new instances, it's possible precisely because of our growing dependence on information to lead our daily lives.

Just as the inexorable cycle of good, bad, and stable has happened at every layer, so it will happen with big data. But unlike attacks on lower levels of the stack, this time it won't just be spam in an inbox. It'll be both our online and offline lives. Attackers can corrupt information, blind an algorithm, inject falsehood, changing outcomes in subtle, insidious ways that undermine a competitor or flip an election. Attacks on data become attacks on people.

If I have to pick a few hot topics for 2013, data warfare is one of them. I'm looking forward to next week's online event (*http://bit.ly/1al76Yz*), because I'm convinced that this arms race will affect all of us in the coming years, and it'll be a long time before the armistice or détente.

Five Big Data Predictions for 2013

Diversity and manageability are big data watchwords for the next 12 months.

By Edd Dumbill (*http://bit.ly/1dpvX7W*)

Here are some of the key big data themes I expect to dominate 2013, and of course will be covering in Strata (*http://oreil.ly/1al7aHH*).

Emergence of a big data architecture

Figure 3-3. Leadenhall Building skyscraper under construction by Martin Pettitt, on Flickr

The coming year will mark the graduation for many big data pilot projects, as they are put into production. With that comes an understanding of the practical architectures that work. These architectures will identify:

- Best-of-breed tools for different purposes; for instance, Storm (*http://bit.ly/1dpwAyc*) for streaming data acquisition
- Appropriate roles for relational databases, Hadoop, NoSQL stores, and in-memory databases
- How to combine existing data warehouses and analytical databases with Hadoop

Of course, these architectures will be in constant evolution as big data tooling matures and experience is gained.

In parallel, I expect to see increasing understanding of where big data responsibility sits within a company's org chart. Big data is fundamentally a business problem, and some of the biggest challenges in taking advantage of it lie in the changes required to cross organizational silos and reforming decision making.

One to watch: it's hard to move data, so look for a starring architectural role in HDFS for the foreseeable future.

Hadoop Is Not the Only Fruit

Though deservedly the poster child for big data software, Hadoop is not the only way to process big data. Credible competitors are emerging, especially where specialized applications are concerned. For example, the Berkeley Data Analytics Stack (*http://bit.ly/1al7aYk*) offers an alternative platform that performs much faster than Hadoop MapReduce for some applications focused on data mining and machine learning.

At the same time, Hadoop is reinventing itself. Hadoop distributions this year will embrace Hadoop 2.0, and in particular YARN (*http://bit.ly/1dpwDtS*), a replacement for the batch-oriented MapReduce part of Hadoop that will permit other kinds of workloads to be executed.

For any big data competitor to get traction, it will need to both be open source and also fully support SQL-like access to data, which became an entry-level requirement over the course of 2012. Hadoop's not going anywhere soon, but a pleasing diversity of tools is emerging.

One to watch: expect to see one or more startups emerging to commercialize the Berkeley Data Analytics Stack.

Turnkey Big Data Platforms

Hadoop has a lot of moving parts. A lot. Even with the administration tools from vendors such as Cloudera and Hortonworks, there's still significant work required in setting up and running a Hadoop cluster. In our age of cloud services, there's no reason that should be so, as demonstrated by Amazon's Elastic MapReduce service.

Expect Hadoop vendors to focus on removing system administration overhead over the course of this year, and other companies providing integrated big data stacks. InfoChimps (*http://bit.ly/1al7bvb*) offers a big data stack managed as a service within private data centers.

For those content to run in the public cloud, Qubole (*http://bit.ly/ 1al5f66*) takes the concept one level further, with a turnkey Hadoop and Hive analysis platform that runs on Amazon EC2.

One to watch: new entries into enterprise Hadoop infrastructure will include WANdisco (*http://bit.ly/1al7cPO*), following their acquisition of AltoStor (*http://bit.ly/1dpwE0T*).

Data Governance Comes into Focus

As big data goes into production, it will need to integrate with the rest of the enterprise. Many of the issues concerned with data governance (*http://bit.ly/1al7eXO*) will rise to the fore, including:

- Data security
- Data consistency
- Reducing data duplication
- Regulatory compliance

One to watch: data security will become a hot topic this year, including approaches to securing Hadoop and databases with fine-grained security, such as Apache Accumulo (*http://bit.ly/1dpwEhm*).

End-to-End Analytic Solutions Emerge

There are far more people who want to access analytic capabilities than have the IT resources to set up their own Hadoop clusters and code for them. For many *big data* applications, the big data comes from outside sources such as Twitter, or GIS data, but the internal data might be reasonably manageable, such as customer or sales data.

This year will see the growth of SaaS analytics platforms, delivered in the cloud for the swipe of a credit card. Web analytics platforms have pioneered the way here. In 2013, Google intends to expand their analytics offering to address "universal analytics," (*http://bit.ly/ 1al7dmV*) a service currently in closed beta test.

The Frankenstein nature of current big data and BI offerings, most often involving gluing Tableau to an underlying database and accompanying ETL work, means that there's a clear gap in the market for compelling end-to-end analytic solutions, especially targeted at marketing applications.

One to watch: the launch of ClearStory Data (*http://bit.ly/1dpwF51*) into public availability in 2013 will provide dynamic competition for analytics incumbents.

Printing Ourselves

At its best, 3D printing can make us more human by making us whole.

By Julie Steele (*http://bit.ly/1al7dTK*)

Tim O'Reilly (*http://oreil.ly/1dpwFBV*) recently asked me and some other colleagues which technology seems most like magic to us. There was a thoughtful pause as we each considered the amazing innovations we read about and interact with every day.

I didn't have to think for long. To me, the thing that seems most like magic isn't Siri (*http://bit.ly/1al7eai*) or self-driving cars (*http://bit.ly/1dpwFSx*) or augmented reality displays (*http://bit.ly/1dpwxTb*). It's 3D printing.

My reasons are different than you might think. Yes, it's amazing that, with very little skill, we can manufacture complex objects in our homes and workshops that are made from things like plastic (*http://bit.ly/1dpwIxy*) or wood (*http://bit.ly/1al7giv*) or chocolate (*http://bit.ly/1dpwGpH*) or even titanium (*http://www.youtube.com/watch?v=E7−ZWPVVdQ*). This seems an amazing act of conjuring that, just a short time ago, would have been difficult to imagine outside of the *Star Trek* set.

But the thing that makes 3D printing really special is the magic it allows us to perform: the technology is capable of making us more human.

I recently had the opportunity to lay out this idea in an Ignite talk at Strata Rx (*http://oreil.ly/1al7gz7*), a new conference on data science and health care that I chaired with Colin Hill. Here's the talk I gave there (*http://bit.ly/1dpwGWG*) (don't worry: like all Ignite (*http://bit.ly/1al7hD9*) talks, it's only five minutes long).

In addition to the applications mentioned in my talk, there are even more amazing accomplishments just over the horizon. Doctor Anthony Atala (*http://bit.ly/1dpwJli*) of the Wake Forest University School of Medicine, recently printed a human kidney onstage at TED (*http://bit.ly/1al7ia2*).

This was not actually a working kidney—one of the challenges to creating working organs is building blood vessels that can provide cells on the inside of the organ structure with nutrients; right now, the cells inside larger structures tend to die rapidly. But researchers at MIT and the University of Pennsylvania are experimenting with printing these vessel networks in sugar (*http://bit.ly/1dpwJSb*). Cells can be grown around the networks, and then the sugar can be dissolved, leaving a void through which blood could flow. As printer resolution improves, these networks can become finer.

And 3D printing becomes even more powerful when combined with other technologies. For example, researchers at the Wake Forest Institute of Regenerative Medicine are using a hybrid 3D printing/electrospinning technique (*http://wrd.cm/1al7iqO*) to print replacement cartilage.

As practiced by Bespoke Innovations (*http://bit.ly/1dpwMNP*), the WREX team (*http://bit.ly/1al7iXI*), and others (*http://bit.ly/1dpwN4p*), 3D printing requires a very advanced and carefully honed skillset; it is not yet within reach of the average DIYer. But what is so amazing—what makes it magic—is that when used in these ways at such a level, the technology disappears. You don't really see it, not unless you're looking. What you see is the person it benefits.

Technology that augments us, that makes us more than we are even at our best (such as self-driving cars or sophisticated digital assistants) is a neat party trick, and an homage to our superheroes. But those that are superhuman are not like us; they are Other. Every story, from *Superman* to the *X-Men* to the *Watchmen*, includes an element of struggle with what it means to be more than human. In short, it means outsider status.

We are never more acutely aware of our own humanity, and all the frailty that entails, as when we are sick or injured. When we can use technology such as 3D printing to make us more whole, then it makes us more human, not Other. It restores our insider status.

Ask anyone who has lost something truly precious and then found it again. I'm talking on the level of an arm, a leg, a kidney, a jaw. If that doesn't seem like magic, then I don't know what does.

Software that Keeps an Eye on Grandma

Networked sensors and machine learning make it easy to see when things are out of the ordinary.

By Jon Bruner (*http://oreil.ly/1al7juM*)

Much of health care—particularly for the elderly—is about detecting change, and, as the mobile health (*http://oreil.ly/1dpwNkW*) movement would have it, computers are very good at that. Given enough sensors, software can model an individual's behavior patterns and then figure out when things are out of the ordinary—when gait slows, posture stoops, or bedtime moves earlier.

Technology already exists (*http://nyti.ms/1al7lCO*) that lets users set parameters for households they're monitoring. Systems are available that send an alert if someone leaves the house in the middle of the night or sleeps past a preset time. Those systems involve context-specific hardware (i.e., a bed-pressure sensor) and conscientious modeling (you have to know what time your grandmother usually wakes up).

The next step would be a generic system. One that, following simple setup, would learn the habits of the people it monitors and then detect the sorts of problems that beset elderly people living alone—falls, disorientation, and so forth—as well as more subtle changes in behavior that could signal other health problems.

A group of researchers from Austria and Turkey has developed just such a system, which they presented at the IEEE's Industrial Electronics Society meeting in Montreal in October.[1]

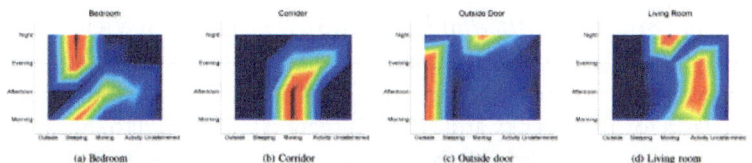

Fig. 2. The extracted high level features. As displayed in Fig. 2a, the bedroom is related with *Sleeping* in the night and in the morning whereas it is related with *Moving* and *Activity* in the afternoon. The corridor is displayed in Fig. 2b and it is related with *Moving* most of the time. It is observed that the model could also locate the outside door as illustrated in Fig. 2c. Finally, the living room, Fig. 2d, is almost always related with *Activity* whereas it is related to *Moving* in the night which makes sense because the person passes through the living room when going to toilet.

1. Available for a fee from IEEE: C. Tirkaz, D. Bruckner, G. Yin, J. Haase, "Activity Recognition Using a Hierarchical Model," Proceedings of the 38th Annual Conference of the IEEE Industrial Electronics Society, pp. 2802–2808, 2012.

In their approach, the researchers train a machine-learning algorithm with several days of routine household activity using door and motion sensors distributed through the living space. The sensors aren't associated with any particular room at the outset: their software algorithmically determines the relative positions of the sensors, then classifies the rooms that they're in based on activity patterns over the course of the day.

From there, it's easy to train software with habits—when bedtime typically occurs, how long an occupant usually spends in the kitchen—though these are handled generically (you don't need to label the bedroom as the bedroom in order for the algorithm to detect that something is amiss when the occupant spends too long there).

The result is somewhat more subtle in its understanding of how a household works and when something might be out of order: if movement in the bedroom between 7 and 8 AM is usually followed by the opening of the bedroom door, then the same movement pattern without the door opening might suggest that someone has fallen while getting out of bed.

The researchers found that, compared to activity manually labeled by test users, their system was accurate at 81% to 87% depending on the type of algorithm used (SVM, CVS, or Hierarchical).

Networks of devices can bring intelligence out of individual machines and into centralized software that can understand an environment in its totality. That's a central part of the philosophy of the industrial Internet (*http://oreil.ly/1dpwNBv*), in which networked machines feed data into sophisticated software that can solve complex optimization problems that take large systems into account.

Dietmar Bruckner (*http://bit.ly/1al7ne5*), a professor at Vienna University of Technology and an author of the paper, says his software (known by the tortured acronym ATTEND—AdapTive scenario recogniTion for Emergency and Need Detection) is tailored to the home-monitoring case outlined in his paper, but it could eventually be generalized to other types of building-monitoring applications.

Asked about bringing the technology to market, Bruckner said his research was being discontinued under funding cutbacks at his university. That's unfortunate given the technology industry's interest in using machine intelligence to deliver better health care. Might this be an opportunity for a startup to pick up where Bruckner et al. leave off?

In the 2012 Election, Big Data-Driven Analysis and Campaigns Were the Big Winners

Data science played a decisive role in the 2012 election, from the campaigns to the coverage

By Alex Howard (*http://bit.ly/1dpweYi*)

On Tuesday night, President Barack Obama was elected to a second term in office. In a world of technology and political punditry (*http://slate.me/1al7nKZ*), the big winner (*http://huff.to/1dpwMgX*) is Nate Silver (*http://bit.ly/1al7pSY*), the *New York Times* blogger at *Five Thirty Eight* (*http://nyti.ms/1dpwOp7*). (Break out your dictionaries: a psephologist (*http://bit.ly/1al7oyG*) is a national figure.)

After he correctly called all 50 states (*http://bit.ly/1dpwOW2*), Silver is being celebrated (*http://huff.to/1dpwMgX*) as the "king of the quants" (*http://cnet.co/1dpwPJL*) by CNET (*http://huff.to/1dpwMgX*) and the "nerdy Chuck Norris" (*http://wrd.cm/1dpwQgI*) by *Wired*. The combined success of statistical models from Silver, TPM PollTracker (*http://bit.ly/1al7syk*), HuffPost Pollster (*http://huff.to/1dpwQNE*), RealClearPolitics Average (*http://bit.ly/1al7sOR*), and the Princeton Election Consortium (*http://bit.ly/1dpwTcf*) all make traditional *horse race journalism* (which uses insider information from the campaign trail to explain what's really going on) look a bit, well, antiquated. With the rise of political data science (*http://huff.to/1al7t5q*), *The Guardian* even went so far as to say that big data may sound the death knell for punditry (*http://bit.ly/1dpwRkQ*).

This election season should serve, in general, as a wake-up call for data-illiterate journalists (*http://bit.ly/1al7tlQ*). It was certainly a triumph of logic over punditry (*http://bit.ly/1dpwRRE*). At this point, it's fair to "predict" that Silver's reputation and the role of data analysis will continue to endure, long after 2012.

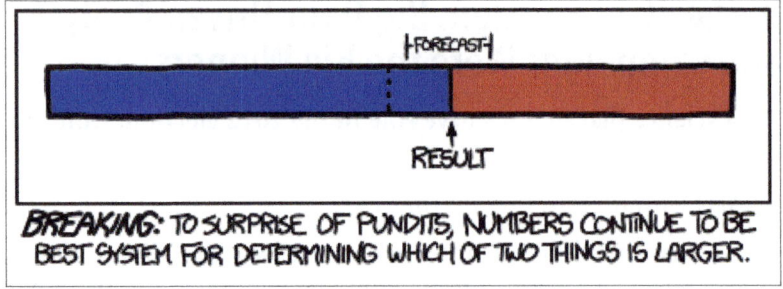

Figure 3-4. "As of this writing, the only thing that's 'razor-thin' or 'too close to call' is the gap between the consensus poll forecast and the result."—Randall Munroe

The Data Campaign

The other big tech story to emerge from the electoral fray, however, is how the campaigns themselves used technology. What social media was to 2008, data-driven campaigning was in 2012. In the wake of this election, people who understand math (*http://bit.ly/1al7vdk*), programming, and data science will be in even higher demand as a strategic advantage in campaigns, from getting out the vote (*http://slate.me/1dpwTZS*) to targeting and persuading voters (*http://slate.me/1al7vdz*).

For political scientists and campaign staff, the story of the quants and data crunchers who helped President Obama win (*http://ti.me/1dpwV3V*) will be pored over and analyzed for years to come. For those wondering how the first big data election played out, Sarah Lai Stirland's analysis of how Obama's digital infrastructure helped him win re-election (*http://bit.ly/1al7x4U*) is a must read, as is Nick Judd's breakdown of former Massachusetts governor Mitt Romney's digital campaign (*http://bit.ly/1dpwUx2*). The Obama campaign found voters (*http://nyti.ms/1al7x59*) in battleground states that their opponents apparently didn't know existed. The exit polls (*http://wapo.st/1dpwXJ3*) suggest that finding and turning out the winning coalition of young people, minorities, and women was critical—and data-driven campaigning clearly played a role.

Tracking the Data Storm Around Hurricane Sandy

When natural disasters loom, public open government data feeds become critical infrastructure.

By Alex Howard (*http://bit.ly/1dpweYi*)

Just over fourteen months ago, social, mapping, and mobile data told the story of Hurricane Irene (*http://oreil.ly/1dpwW7S*). As a larger, more unusual late October storm churns its way up the East Coast, the people in its path are once again acting as sensors (*http://oreil.ly/1dpwW7S*) and media, creating crisis data as this "Frankenstorm" (*http://bit.ly/1dpwWov*) moves over them.

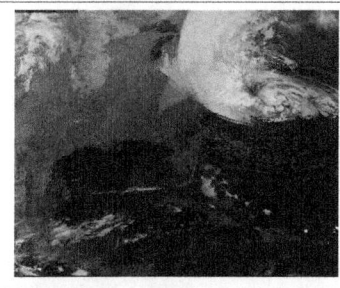

Figure 3-5. Hurricane Sandy is seen on the east coast of the United States in this NASA handout satellite image taken at 0715 GMT, October 29, 2012 (Photo Credit: NASA)

As citizens look for hurricane information online, government websites are under high demand. In late 2012, media, government, the private sector, and citizens all now will play an important role in sharing information about what's happening and providing help to one another.

In that context, it's key to understand that it's government weather data, gathered and shared from satellites high above the Earth, that's being used by a huge number of infomediaries to forecast, predict, and instruct people about what to expect and what to do. In perhaps the most impressive mashup of social and government data now online, an interactive Google Crisis Map for Hurricane Sandy (*http://bit.ly/1al7wOu*) pictured below predicts the future of the "Frankenstorm" (*http://bit.ly/1dpwYNd*) in real time, including a New York City-specific version (*http://bit.ly/1al7zK8*).

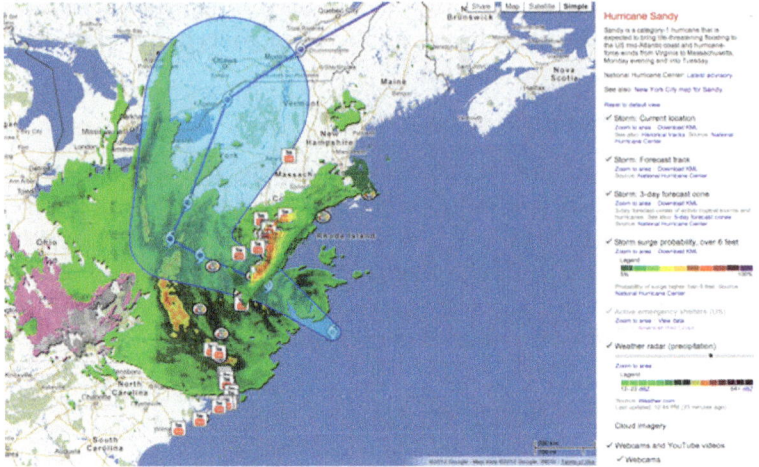

If you're looking for a great example of public data for public good (*http://bit.ly/1dpwZke*), these maps, like the Weather Underground's (*http://bit.ly/1al7yGc*) interactive, are a canonical example of what's possible.

Matt Lira, the digital director for the Majority Leader in the U.S. House of Representatives, made an important, clear connection between open government, weather data, and a gorgeous wind visualization (*http://bit.ly/1dpwZRc*) passed around today.

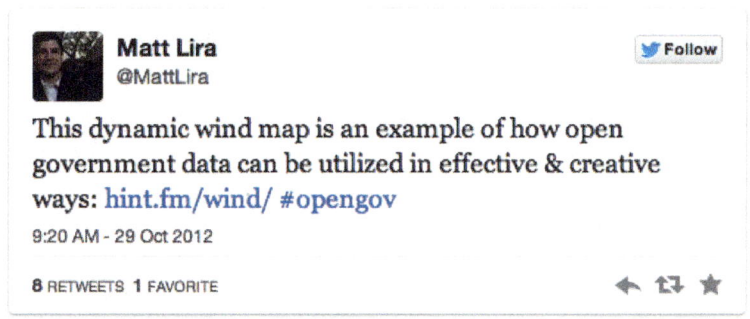

(In the context of the utility of weather data, it will be interesting to see if Congress takes action to fund weather satellite replacements (*http://bit.ly/1al7yWN*).)

In New York City, as the city's websites faced heavy demand when residents went to its hurricane evacuation finder (*http://on.nyc.gov/1dpx0oe*) on Sunday, residents could also go and consult WNYC's beautiful evacuation map. (Civiguard also activated an instant evacuation zone checker (*http://bit.ly/1al7zdg*) for smartphones and modern browsers.) WNYC data news editor (*http://bit.ly/1dpx3k1*) John Keefe is responsible for the map below that puts the city's open government data in action.

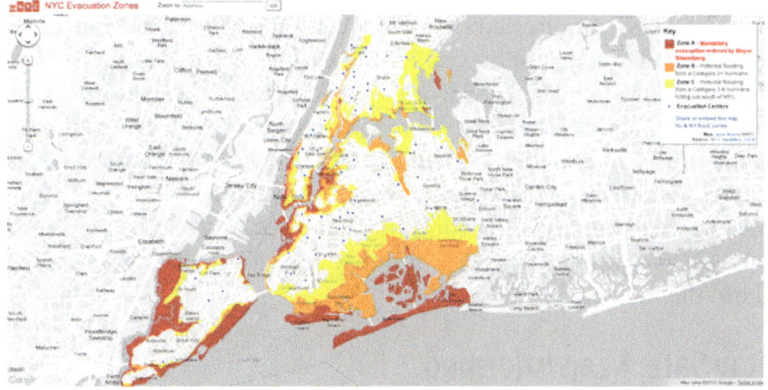

By releasing open data for use in these apps, New York City and the U.S. federal government are acting as a platform for public media, civic entrepreneurs, and nonprofits to enable people to help themselves and one another at a crucial time. When natural disasters loom, public data feeds can become critical infrastructure.

For one more example of how this looks in practice, look at WNYC's storm surge map (*http://wny.cc/1al7AO8*) for New York and New Jersey.

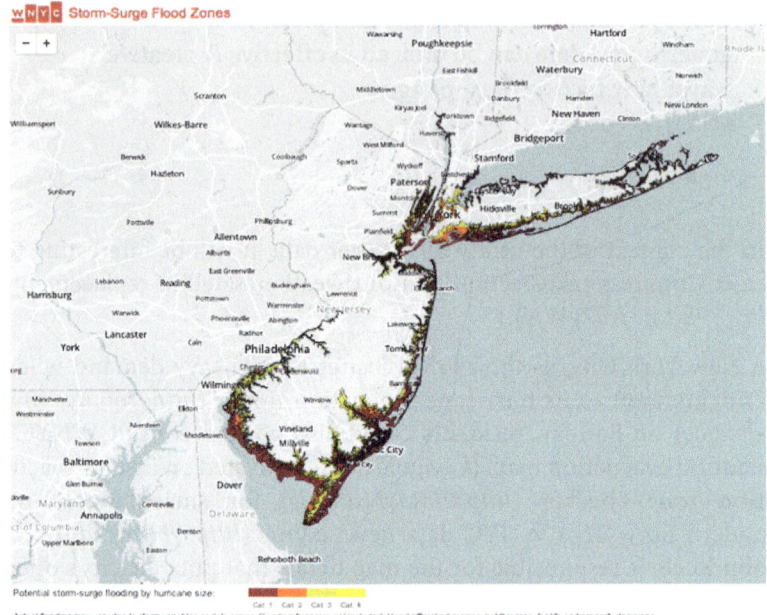

If you're a coder interested in working with the tech community, MIT Media Lab Director Joi Ito (*http://bit.ly/1dpx1bL*) is helping to coordinate #HurricaneHackers working on projects and resources for Hurricane Sandy (*http://bit.ly/hurricanehackers-gdoc*). The group has made a timeline of events (*http://bit.ly/hurricanehackers-sandytimeline-test*), a list of livestreams (*http://bit.ly/1al7CWw*), along with aggregating links to official data and social streams, like Instacane (*http://bit.ly/1dpx47u*), a site that aggregates Instagram images about the hurricane.

Stay Safe, Keep Informed

Hurricane Sandy has meteorologists scared (*http://bit.ly/1al7Dtk*), and for good reason. The federal government is providing information on Hurricane Sandy at Hurricanes.gov (*http://1.usa.gov/1dpx4o4*) and NOAA (*http://1.usa.gov/1al7BBY*), and sharing news and advisories in real-time on the radio, television, mobile devices, and online using social media channels like @FEMA (*http://bit.ly/1dpx4UV*).

As the storm comes in, FEMA recommends http://m.fema.gov/ (*http://1.usa.gov/1al7BSp*) to mobile users and http://ready.gov/ (*http://1.usa.gov/1dpx2wr*) for desktops. The *Wall Street Journal* (*http://on.wsj.com/1al7Eh4*) and Reuters (*http://bit.ly/1dpx87c*) are both live-blogging the news. Like WNYC, the Associated Press (*http://apne.ws/1al7ENT*) and Reuters used weather data to populate interactive Hurricane Tracker (*http://reut.rs/1dpx5IG*) maps.

People in the path of the storm can download smartphone apps from the Red Cross (*http://rdcrss.org/R4gjDV*) and FEMA (*http://bit.ly/ToDgqB*) on Android, iOS (*http://bit.ly/sNZNJI*), or BlackBerry (*http://bit.ly/wUiqHL*).

If you do not have a smartphone, save 43362 (4FEMA) to your mobile phone and charge it up. If, after #Sandy, you cannot return home and have immediate housing needs, text SHELTER + zip code to 43362.

A Grisly Job for Data Scientists

Matching the missing to the dead involves reconciling two national databases.

By Jon Bruner (*http://oreil.ly/1al7juM*)

Javier Reveron went missing from Ohio in 2004. His wallet turned up in New York City, but he was nowhere to be found. By the time his parents arrived to search for him and hand out fliers, his remains had already been buried in an unmarked indigent grave. In New York, where coroner's resources are precious, remains wait a few months to be claimed before they're buried by convicts in a potter's field on uninhabited Hart Island (*http://bit.ly/1dpx8Ek*), just off the Bronx in Long Island Sound.

The story (*http://nyti.ms/1al7FS8*), reported by the *New York Times* last week, has as happy an ending as it could given that beginning. In 2010, Reveron's parents added him to a national database of missing persons. A month later police in New York matched him to an unidentified body and his remains were disinterred, cremated, and given burial ceremonies in Ohio.

Reveron's ordeal suggests an intriguing, and impactful, machine-learning problem. The Department of Justice maintains separate national public databases for missing people (*http://bit.ly/1dpx8UJ*), unidentified people (*http://bit.ly/1al7I0m*), and unclaimed people (*http://bit.ly/1dpx9bi*). Many records are full of rich data that is almost never a perfect match to data in other databases—hair color entered by a police department might differ from how it's remembered by a missing person's family; weights fluctuate; scars appear. Photos are provided for many missing people and some unidentified people, and matching them is difficult. Free-text fields in many entries describe the circumstances under which missing people lived and died; a predilection for hitchhiking could be linked to a death by the side of a road.

I've called the Department of Justice (DOJ) to ask about the extent to which they've worked with computer scientists to match missing and unidentified people, and will update when I hear back. One thing that's not immediately apparent is the public availability of the necessary training set—cases that have been successfully matched and removed from the lists. The DOJ apparently doesn't comment on resolved cases, which could make getting this data difficult. But perhaps there's room for a coalition to request the anonymized data and manage it to the DOJ's satisfaction while distributing it to capable data scientists.

Health Care

Big data established its footing in the health care industry in 2013. This chapter looks at the increasing role data is playing in genetics, genomics, diagnosing conditions, personal health care monitoring and disease prevention, and in health care system modeling.

Would you share information about your dandruff condition if it would help researchers find a cure for lupus? What if by doing so, researchers ultimately were able to identify you—and your medical conditions—from your genomic data? In "Genomics and Privacy at the Crossroads" on page 163, James Turner takes a look at the Personal Genome Project and its Open Consent model, and examines privacy concerns inherent therein. Crowdsourcing data also is playing a role in drug discovery, as Andy Oram investigates in "A Very Serious Game That Can Cure the Orphan Diseases" on page 167. Oram also takes a look at Harvard's SMART health care apps, and offers a two-part series reporting from Sage Congress.

Government agencies are making use of big data on the health care front as well: Julie Steele delves into the CDC's open content APIs in "Making Government Health Data Personal Again" on page 173, and Oram, in "Driven to Distraction: How Veterans Affairs Uses Monitoring Technology to Help Returning Veterans" on page 177, looks how the Sprout device is helping veterans by collecting and analyzing sensor data in real time.

And it's no secret that individuals are increasingly collecting and using their personal health data to put themselves in the driver's seat, whether to assist in diagnoses and treatment or to adopt and monitor healthier behaviors in efforts of disease prevention. Linda Stone takes a look at the quantified self movement and suggests it could go a bit further in "Quantified Self to Essential Self: Mind and Body as Partners in Health" on page 185.

Moving to the Open Health-Care Graph

A network graph approach to modeling the health care system.

By Fred Trotter (*http://bit.ly/1iKEbQ2*)

To achieve the triple aim (*http://bit.ly/1dpx7jJ*) in health care (better, cheaper, and safer), we are going to need intensive monitoring and measurement of specific doctors, hospitals, labs, and countless other clinical professionals and clinical organizations. We need specific data and specific doctors.

In 1979 (*http://bit.ly/1al7INC*), a Federal judge in Florida sided with the AMA to prevent these kinds of provider-specific data sets, deciding that they violated doctor privacy. Last Friday, a different Florida judge reversed the 1979 injunction, allowing provider-identified data to be released from CMS under FOIA requests. Even without this tremendous victory for the *Wall Street Journal* (*http://on.wsj.com/1dpx9Iq*), there was already a shift away from aggregation studies in health care toward using big data methods on specific doctors to improve health care. This critical shift will allow us to determine which doctors are doing the best job, and which are doing the worst. We can target struggling doctors to help improve care, and we can also target the best doctors, so we can learn new best practices in health care.

Evidence-based medicine must be targeted to handle specific clinical contexts. The only really open questions to decide are "how much data should we release" and "should this be done in secret or in the open." I submit that the targeting should be done at the individual and team levels, and that this must be an open process. We need to start tracking the performance and clinical decisions of specific doctors working with other specific doctors, in a way that allows for public scrutiny. We need to release uncomfortably personal data about specific physicians and evaluate that data in a fair manner, without sparking a witch hunt. And whether you agree with this approach or not, it's already underway. The overturning of this court case will only open the flood gates further.

Last year, I released DocGraph at Strata RX (*http://bit.ly/1al7INS*). DocGraph details how specific doctors and hospitals team together to deliver health care (data on referral patterns, etc.). At that conference, we (Not Only Development (*http://bit.ly/1dpxaMs*)) promised that this data set would go open source eventually. This month, we will be announcing that the DocGraph data set is available for costless download. But there are two other data sets that can now be used to make that graph data much richer.

Graph or *network* data, in this context, refers to a computing technique that represents nodes (in this case doctors, hospitals, etc.) connected by edges (in this case, representing which doctors and hospitals work together). So DocGraph explicitly states that Dr. Smith (a primary care doctor) is working with Dr. Jones (a cardiologist), and assigns a strength to that relationship.

In order to take a network graph approach to modeling the health care system, you have to name names. We have had specific and incriminating data on US hospitals (*http://1.usa.gov/1al7GW6*) for years now. This openness has been at the heart of a revolution in the field of patient safety (*http://bit.ly/1dpxbjn*). I believe that this openness has been a central motivator for the ongoing reduction of *never events*, perhaps even more important than corresponding payment reforms. On some cases, I even have data (*http://bit.ly/1al7HcI*) to back this assertion.

I am a devotee of new thinking about human motivation (*http://bit.ly/1dpxbzX*), and I believe very strongly that most doctors, even the "bad" ones, want to be the best they can at what they do, largely independent of financial incentives. But doctors need uncomfortably personal data on how they, specifically, are doing in order to start doing it better.

This has been the month for the open release of uncomfortably personal data about the health care system.

First, HHS announced the release of data on master charge sets for hospitals. This is likely a direct response to the problems with master charge sets in the masterful "Bitter Pill: Why Medical Bills Are Killing Us" (*http://ti.me/1al7JRO*) article by Steven Brill in *Time* magazine. The data released by CMS (*http://go.cms.gov/1dpxbQx*) is a complex data set about an even more complex medico-legal issue, but a useful oversimplification is this: it shows which hospitals have been the worst abusers of cash-paying, uninsured patients. You could write entire articles (*http://ti.me/1al7K8q*) about the structure, value, and depth of this data set…and I plan to, given infinite time and resources.

But then, in the midst of this, ProPublica released data on the prescribing patterns of almost every doctor in the United States (*http://bit.ly/1dpxcnr*). This is detailed information about the preferences of almost every doctor who participates in the Medicare Part D prescription program, which is almost every doctor. Does your doctor prefer Oxycontin to Vicodin? Which antibiotic does your doctor use most frequently? These choices, taken together, can be called a "prescribing pattern." ProPublica is allowing the public to view those patterns for specific doctors.

These data sets are having a combinatorial impact for those of us who are interested in researching the health care system.

Now you can see if your doctor is a conservative (0 (*http://bit.ly/1al7Nko*) 1 (*http://bit.ly/1dpxcDV*) 2 (*http://bit.ly/1al7NkH*) 3 (*http://bit.ly/1al7NkH*) 4 (*http://bit.ly/1al7NRy*) 5 (*http://bit.ly/1al7NRy*)) or a liberal (1 (*http://bit.ly/1al7O8f*) 2 (*http://bit.ly/1dpxgne*) 3 (*http://bit.ly/1al7Mgy*)) prescriber, and you can see if they refer (*http://bit.ly/1dpxgDK*) patients to a hospital that charges more than double what the one across the street does (*http://wapo.st/1al7Mx4*).

Taken together, these changes in data release policy represent two important shifts in the analysis of the healthcare system. We are moving from proprietary analysis to open analysis and from aggregate data to graph (network) data. These moves parallel past scientific process breakthroughs:

Proprietary science → open science
    Illustrated by the move from alchemy to chemistry. Alchemists were famous for doing work in secret, hoping to learn and horde the secrets for turning lead into gold or the secret to eternal life. Chemistry began when researchers gave up secrecy and started sharing important results openly.

Aggregate models → network models
    Illustrated by the move from chromosomal models of genetic inheritance to -omic (*http://bit.ly/1dpxgUh*) (genomic, proteomic, etc.) network models of genetic inheritance. Mendel could spot patterns in the colors of his peas because those genes operated on the chromosomal level. The chromosome acts as a natural phenotypical aggregator for much more complex genetic processes. But that aggregation limits what can be studied. The discovery of DNA allowed researchers to start analyzing inheritance using network models.

For years, there has been a proprietary market for data about how doctors behave, specifically around prescribing patterns. IMS, for instance, is a leading data vendor (*http://bit.ly/1al7PsN*) for this information. If you wanted to purchase prescribing or referral pattern data, IMS will happily provide it (hint: you can't afford it). Despite the high barrier to access, IMS's service has been very unpopular with doctors, and the AMA successfully lobbied for a mechanism that would allow for a doctor to opt out of these prescribing databases (*http://bit.ly/1dpxjiT*). So there is a well-established data vendor community here, with some recent big data entrants.

Two companies using big data graph analysis methods on doctor data have had high-profile funding events. Activate Networks was funded for $10 million in series B (*http://bit.ly/1al7PZO*) and Kyruus received $11 million in series B (*http://bit.ly/1dpxjzt*). The list of people at Kyruus (*http://bit.ly/1al7SVt*) and people at Activate Networks (*http://bit.ly/1dpxk6y*) are filled with the rock stars of this nascent industry who have published seminal papers in the field (*http://1.usa.gov/1al7Tsi*). However, like IMS, these companies are pursuing a proprietary data approach to graph analysis of the health care system.

This is not necessarily by choice—most doctor data is released reluctantly by data owners. They are concerned with ensuring that doctor data does not spill into the public domain. In order to run their businesses, IMS, Activate, and Kyruus have likely made contractual promises that require them to keep of much of the data that they have access to private. In short, these companies are "behind the curtain" of health care informatics. They get substantial benefits by having access to this kind of private health care data and they must accept certain limitations in its use. My limited interactions with these companies has shown that they are as enthusiastic about open data in health care as I am.

When even proprietary players want to shift to more open accountable data models, it is fair to say that this shift is widely accepted. As a society, it is critical for us to move this graph health care data, as much as possible, into the open. This will allow data scientists from IMS, Activate, Kyruus, and others to collaborate with journalists, academics and the open source developer community to make doctor and hospital performance into an open science. HHS has done its part by proactively releasing new critical data sets and by electing not to fight FOIA requests that seek even more data. This is substantive evidence that the mission of open data (*http://1.usa.gov/1dpxkDy*), inspired by

President Obama and implemented by federal CTO Todd Park, is a reality.

The second shift is away from aggregate models for health care researchers. While ProPublica, Kyruus, and Activate have the big data chops to lead this shift, the rank and file health care researcher still routinely uses aggregate data to analyze the health care system as the method of choice. This is true of academic researchers, health care industry administrators, and policy makers alike. Understanding statistics is really the first step towards being a well-rounded data scientist, but it is only the first step.

Traditional statistical approaches, like traditional economic approaches, are powerful because they make certain simplifying assumptions about the world. Like many generalizations, they are useful cognitive shortcuts until they are too frequently proven untrue. There is no *normal* prescribing pattern, for instance, to which a given provider can be judged.

Using averages across zip code, city, state, or regional boundaries is a useful way to detect and describe the problems that we have in health care. But it is a terrible way to create feedback and control loops. An infectious disease clinic, for instance, will be unperturbed to learn that it has higher rate of infection scores than neighboring clinics. In fact, they are a magnet for infection cases, and hopefully should have higher infection case loads, but a lower infection rates. Many scoring systems are unable to make these kinds of distinctions. Similarly, a center for cancer excellence would not be surprised to learn that they have shorter life span scores than other cancer treatment centers. Any last resort clinical center would show those effects, as they attract the most difficult cases.

It is difficult to use averages, scores, and other simplistic mathematical shortcuts to detect real problems in health care. We need a new norm where the average health care researcher's initial tool of choice is Gephi (*http://bit.ly/1a1opc5*) rather than Excel and Neo4J (*http://bit.ly/1dpxlHu*) rather than SQL. The aggregate approach has taken the health care system this far, but we need to have deeper understandings of how the health care system works—and fails—if we want to achieve the triple aim. We need models that incorporate details about specific doctors and hospitals. We need to move from simplistic mathematical shortcuts to complex mathematical models; big data if you like that term.

We need to have both shifts at the same time. It is not enough to have the shift to open data, in aggregate, or the shift to network models trapped behind the insiders curtain. That has been happening for years and this creates troubling power dynamics. When the public can see only averages but the insiders get to see the graph of health care, we will enjoy only narrow optimizations and limited uses.

Currently, there is no simple way for data scientists at an EHR company, an insurance company, and a drug company to teach each other how to better leverage the health care graph. Each of these companies has a lens on the *true* graph created using only a slice of the relevant data. But the limitations of the data are really the least of the problems facing these researchers working in isolation. For each data scientist, working in isolation, there is no way to generally test hypotheses with outsiders. There is no way to "stand back and try science" (*http://bit.ly/1al7RAQ*) because science is a community process.

We need to create a community of health care graph researchers and provide that community with the nonaggregate data it needs to create the algorithms that will dictate how medicine operates for the next century. This is not a project for any single company to take on; we are betting too much as a society to have that kind of pressure. No company or data scientist I know of even wants that kind of role. Instead, every company in the space is interested in leveraging and contributing open data, so that the hypothesis and methods developed behind the curtain can be validated in the open.

Before the release of these three data sets, data scientists were in the tremendously uncomfortable position of having to make critical business decisions while being only "probably right." Given the ease with which "probably right" can turn into "completely wrong" (*http://bit.ly/1dpxlHI*) with data, we should work hard to ensure that data scientists are not put in this position again.

Genomics and Privacy at the Crossroads

Would you let people know about your dandruff problem if it might mean a cure for Lupus?

By James Turner (*http://bit.ly/1al7Uwm*)

Two weeks ago, I had the privilege to attend the 2013 Genomes, Environments, and Traits (GET) Conference (*http://bit.ly/1dpxomR*) in Boston, as a participant of Harvard Medical School's Personal Genome

Project. Several hundreds of us attended the conference, eager to learn what new breakthroughs might be in the works using the data and samples we have contributed, and to network with the researchers and each other.

The Personal Genome Project (PGP) (*http://bit.ly/1al7XIC*) is a very different type of beast from the traditional research study model in several ways. To begin with, it is an *open consent* (*http://bit.ly/1dpxmeH*) study, which means that all the data that participants donate is available for research by anyone without further consent by the subject. In other words, having initially consented to participate in the PGP, anyone can download my genome sequence, look at my phenotypic traits (my physical characteristics and medical history), or even order some of my blood from a cell line that has been established at the Coriell biobank (*http://bit.ly/1al7XZ3*), and they do not need to gain specific consent from me to do so. By contrast, in most research studies, data and samples can only be collected for one specific study, and no other purposes. This is all in an effort to protect the privacy of the participants, as was famously violated in the establishment of the HeLa (*http://bit.ly/1dpxmv6*) cell line.

The other big difference is that in most studies, the participants rarely receive any information back from the researchers. For example, if the researcher does a brain MRI to gather data about the structure of a part of your brain, and sees a huge tumor, they are under no obligation to inform you about it, or even to give you a copy of the scan. This is because researchers are not certified as clinical laboratories, and thus are not authorized to report medical findings. This makes sense, to a certain extent, with traditional medical tests, as the research version may not be calibrated to detect the same things, and the researcher is not qualified to interpret the results for medical purposes.

But this model falls apart when you are talking about Whole Genome Sequencing (WGS). In most cases, the sequencing done by a researcher is done in the same facility that a commercial clinical laboratory would use. And a WGS isn't like a traditional medical test; it's a snapshot of your entire genetic makeup, and contains a wealth of information that has nothing to do with whatever a specific researcher may be investigating. Shouldn't you know if a WGS ordered by a researcher to look at autism also discovers that you have one of the *bad* BRCA1 mutations for breast cancer?

Historically, the high cost of WGS has made the problem largely academic, but not anymore. The cost of WGS in bulk is now approaching or under $2,000, with $1,000 expected to be the going rate very shortly. At this kind of price, it becomes an invaluable tool for scientists looking for links between genetic mutations and particular traits (good and bad). They can use a technique called a Genome Wide Association Study (GWAS) to search for correlations between changes in DNA and diseases, for example.

The increasing use of GWAS is precisely why the PGP and its open consent model was created. Suppose you have 20 people who all have had gallstones, and you want to find out if they all share a common mutation. Because there are so many random mutations in our DNA, there are likely to be a large number of mutations that they will share by happenstance. What you need is a large control population without gallstones, so that you can rule out mutations that occur in people who have not gone on to develop the condition. There are databases that tell you how often a mutation occurs in the general public, but they don't tell you how often they occur in people without gallstones. Because the PGP participants have not only consented to have their data used by anyone who wants to, but have (and continue to) contribute a rich set of phenotypic trait data, you can find PGP members who have or have not developed stones, and download their genomes.

The price that PGP members ask for the free and open use of their existing data is that new data be returned to the PGP members and made available for others to use. For example, I'll be getting copies of my brain MRI and uploading them to my PGP profile, and the data on my microbiome (the bacteria in my gut and on my skin) has already been placed there by the University of Colorado's American Gut (*http://bit.ly/1al7Vk4*) research project. Not only does this let other researchers gain access to the new data, but it lets the more curious of the PGP participants learn things about themselves (woohoo, 3.2% of my stool bacteria is Ruminococcus!). One of the things that PGP members have to agree to is the understanding that any data they receive is not to be used for diagnostic purposes, although in practice several participants have used their PGP WGS data to determine the cause of illnesses that they had suffered from without explanations.

The future of GWAS, and genomic research in general, rests on the availability of a rich and diverse group of participants willing to serve as controls and cases for new studies, without the researchers having to go to the effort and cost of *consenting* the study sample each and every time. The goal of the PGP is to eventually enroll 100,000 members, to help meet this need.

But there's a larger issue lurking beyond the question of consent, and that deals with privacy. There's not much likelihood that a researcher or other entity could identify you from an MRI scan of your brain, but as public databases of genomic data grow, the chance that at least your surname can be intuited from your genome is becoming more of a fact (*http://bit.ly/1dpxpHc*) than a possibility. This was demonstrated at GET 2013, along with the fact that with only three pieces of data (age, gender, and zip code), it is almost always possible to narrow down to a single individual using publicly available data. At a minimum, this means that someone with your genome and a list of your traits is in a good position to link you to your medical problems, which could cause a problem when applying for life insurance (as an example). It gets more complex still if you imagine what would happen if some seriously detrimental mutation is discovered at a later date. Suppose it was suddenly common knowledge that you had an allele that was strongly linked to psychopathy?

As a result, the PGP participants have recently been given notice by the project researchers that they should no longer depend on the expectation of privacy at all. All of the participants knew this risk going in, as it was explicitly spelled out as part of the original test that you had to pass in order to participate, but it's now the reality on the ground. Rather than cling to the hope that they will remain anonymous, many PGP members have publicly revealed their PGP identifiers (I'm PGP65 (*http://bit.ly/1al7VAv*) for example, should you wish to learn about my valiant battle with gallstones revealed in my phenotypic data), and the project is considering adding photos and real names as optional data available on PGP records.

As we learned at the conference, in the Canadian version of the PGP there are essentially no concerns about privacy. Canada, in fact, lacks even the minimal protections that GINA (*http://1.usa.gov/1dpxn25*) provides in the United States. But since Canada is a single-payer health care system, the concern that a mutation might be considered a pre-existing condition is eliminated, which evidently provides enough reassurance to Canadians that they are willing to share their genetic data. This is in spite of the risks of job or life insurance discrimination, both of which are possible in Canada at the moment.

So where does this leave us? The reality of WGS, which will probably be as routinely ordered as a chest X-ray within a few years, is upon us. Because of the ability of our genetic data to uniquely identify us, and the way that big data is now linking more and more of our life into a common thread, the day may not be too far off when you get a pop-up ad on your browser advertising a cure of a disease you didn't even know you had. We can either choose to embrace our lack of privacy, as the PGP members are doing, trading it for greater insight into ourselves and the potential to help improve the quality of life for others, or we can try to put the genie back in the bottle.

A Very Serious Game That Can Cure the Orphan Diseases

Fit2Cure taps the public's visual skills to match compounds to targets

By Andy Oram (*http://bit.ly/1al6d2a*)

In the inspiring tradition of Foldit (*http://bit.ly/1dpxn2e*), the game for determining protein shapes, Fit2Cure (*http://bit.ly/1al7W7w*) crowdsources the problem of finding drugs that can cure the many under-researched diseases of developing countries. Fit2Cure appeals to the player's visual—even physical—sense of the world, and requires much less background knowledge than Foldit.

There are about 7,000 rare diseases, fewer than 5% of which have cures. The number of people currently engaged in making drug discoveries is by no means adequate to study all these diseases. A recent gift to Harvard (*http://bit.ly/1dpxquM*) shows the importance that medical researchers attach to filling the gap. As an alternative approach, abstracting the drug discovery process into a game could empower thousands, if not millions, of people to contribute to this process and make discoveries in diseases that get little attention to scientists or pharmaceutical companies.

The biological concept behind Fit2Cure is that medicines have specific shapes that fit into the proteins of the victim's biological structures like jigsaw puzzle pieces (but more rounded). Many cures require finding a drug that has the same jigsaw shape and can fit into the target protein molecule, thus preventing it from functioning normally.

But there are millions of possible medications, and it's hard computationally to figure out which medication can disable which target protein. The way forward may be to tap the human ability to solve (and enjoy solving) jigsaw puzzles.

Fit2Cure therefore presents the user with the shape of the target protein (the common representation called the van der Waals surface) and the shape of a medication. The player can easily and quickly rotate the two molecules and search for places where they fit. The molecules can be rendered partly transparent to help the player see the internal shape he or she is trying to fit.

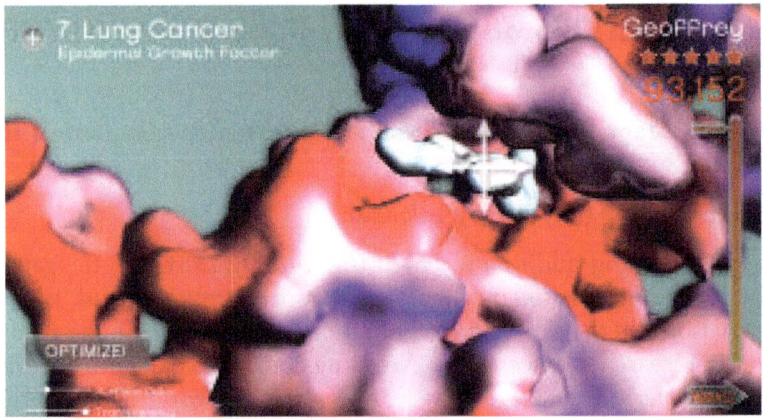

The game was developed by a team led by Geoffrey Siwo, a PhD student at University of Notre Dame and an IBM PhD scholarship award recipient. It is one of the efforts of Sayansia (*http://bit.ly/1al7Wo4*), which Siwo founded together with Ian Sander and Victoria Lam, also PhD students at the University of Notre Dame. Sayansia is derived from the Swahili word sayansi, which means science, and their motto is "Scientific discovery through gaming." The game development was done in conjunction with the serious games company, DynamoidApps (*http://bit.ly/1dpxqLw*) based in Seattle, WA, USA. To play the game, you need to download the Unity Web player.

Data Sharing Drives Diagnoses and Cures, If We Can Get There (Part 1)

Observations from Sage Congress and collaboration through its challenge

By Andy Oram (*http://bit.ly/1al6d2a*)

The glowing reports we read of biotech advances almost cause one's brain to ache. They leave us thinking that medical researchers must command the latest in all technological tools. But the engines of genetic and pharmaceutical innovation are stuttering for lack of one key fuel: data. Here they are left with the equivalent of trying to build skyscrapers with lathes and screwdrivers.

Sage Congress (*http://bit.ly/1dpxr1R*), held this past week in San Francisco, investigated the multiple facets of data in these fields: gene sequences, models for finding pathways, patient behavior, and symptoms (known as phenotypic data), and code to process all these inputs. A survey of efforts by the organizers, Sage Bionetworks (*http://bit.ly/1al7Z3m*), and other innovations in genetic data handling can show how genetics resembles and differs from other disciplines.

An Intense Lesson in Code Sharing

At last year's Congress, Sage announced a challenge, together with the DREAM project (*http://bit.ly/1dpxtXw*), intended to galvanize researchers in genetics while showing off the growing capabilities of Sage's Synapse (*http://bit.ly/1al7XbE*) platform. Synapse ties together a number of data sets in genetics and provides tools for researchers to upload new data, while searching other researchers' data sets. Its challenge highlighted the industry's need for better data sharing, and some ways to get there.

The Sage Bionetworks/DREAM Breast Cancer Prognosis Challenge (*http://bit.ly/1dpxrz1*) was cleverly designed to demonstrate both Synapse's capabilities and the value of sharing. The goal was to find a better way to predict the chances of survival among victims of breast cancer. This is done through computational models that search for patterns in genetic material.

To participate, competing teams had to upload models to Synapse, where they were immediately evaluated against a set of test data and ranked in their success in predicting outcomes. Each team could go online at any time to see who was ahead and examine the code used by the front-runners. Thus, teams could benefit from their competitors' work. The value of Synapse as a cloud service was also manifest. The process is reminiscent of the collaboration among teams to solve the Netflix prediction challenge (*http://wrd.cm/1al7ZAp*).

Although this ability to steal freely from competing teams would seem to be a disincentive to participation, more than 1,400 models were submitted, and the winning model (which was chosen by testing the front-runners against another data set assembled by a different research team in a different time and place) seems to work better then existing models, although it will still have to be tested in practice.

The winner's prize was a gold coin in the currency recognized by researchers: publication in the prestigious journal *Science Translational Medicine* (*http://bit.ly/1dpxuuy*), which agreed in advance to recognize the competition as proof of the value of the work (although the article also went through traditional peer review). Supplementary materials were also posted online to fulfill the Sage mission of promoting reproducibility as well as reuse in new experiments.

Synapse as a Platform

Synapse is a cloud-based service, but is open source so that any organization can store its own data on servers of its choice and provide Synapse-like access. This is important because genetic data sets tend to be huge, and therefore hard to copy. On its own cloud servers, Synapse stores metadata, such as data annotations and provenance information, on data objects that can be located anywhere. This allows organizations to store data on their own servers, while still using the Synapse services. Of course, because Synapse is open source, an organization could also choose to create their own instance, but this would eliminate some of the cross-fertilization across people and projects that has made the code-hosting site GitHub so successful.

Sage rents space on Amazon Web Services, so it looks for AWS solutions, such as DynamoDB for its nonrelational storage area, to fashion each element of Synapse's solution. More detail about Synapse's purpose and goals can be found in my report from last year's Congress (*http://bit.ly/1al80nJ*).

A follow-up to this posting will summarize and compare some ways that the field of genetics is sharing data, and how it is being used both within research and to measure the researchers' own value.

Data Sharing Drives Diagnoses and Cures, If We Can Get There (Part 2)

How the field of genetics is using data within research and to evaluate researchers

By Andy Oram (*http://bit.ly/1al6d2a*)

Data sharing is not an unfamiliar practice in genetics. Plenty of cell lines and other data stores are publicly available from such places as the TCGA data set from the National Cancer Institute (*http://1.usa.gov/1al80nX*), Gene Expression Omnibus (GEO) (*http://1.usa.gov/1dpxuLf*), and Array Expression (*http://bit.ly/1al80Eo*) (all of which can be accessed through Synapse). So to some extent the current revolution in sharing lies not in the data itself but in critical related areas.

First, many of the data sets are weakened by metadata problems. A Sage programmer told me that the famous TCGA set is enormous but poorly curated. For instance, different data sets in TCGA may refer to the same drug by different names, generic versus brand name. *Provenance* (a clear description of how the data was collected and prepared for use) is also weak in TCGA.

In contrast, GEO records tend to contain good provenance information (see an example (*http://1.usa.gov/1dpxvi4*)), but only as free-form text, which presents the same barriers to searching and aggregation as free-form text in medical records. Synapse is developing a structured format for presenting provenance based on the W3C's PROV standard (*http://bit.ly/1al80UP*). One researcher told me this was the most promising contribution of Synapse toward the shared use of genetic information.

Data can also be inaccessible to researchers because it reflects the diversity of patient experiences. One organizer of Army of Women, an organization that collects information from breast cancer patients, says it's one of the largest available data repositories for this disease, but is rarely used because researchers cannot organize it.

Fragmentation in the field of genetics extends to nearly everything that characterizes data. One researcher told me about his difficulties combining the results of two studies, each comparing responses of the same genetic markers to the same medications, because the doses they compared were different.

The very size of data is a barrier. One speaker surveyed all the genotypic information that we know plays a role in creating disease. This includes not only the patient's genome—already many gigabytes of information—but other material in the cell and even the parasitic bacteria that occupy our bodies. All told, he estimated that a complete record of our bodies would require a yottabyte of data, far beyond the capacity of any organization to store.

Synapse tries to make data easier to reuse by encouraging researchers to upload the code they use to manipulate the data. Still, this code may be hard to understand and adapt to new research. Most researchers learn a single programming language such as R or MATLAB and want only code in that language, which in turn restricts the data sets they're willing to use.

Sage has clearly made a strategic choice here to gather as much data and code as possible by minimizing the burden on the researcher when uploading these goods. That puts more burden on the user of the data and code to understand what's on Synapse. A Sage programmer told me that many sites with expert genetics researchers lack programming knowledge. This has to change.

Measure Your Words

Standardized data can transform research far beyond the lab, including the critical areas of publication and attribution. Current scientific papers bear large strings of authors—what did each author actually contribute? The last author is often a chief scientist who did none of the experimentation or writing on the paper, but organized and directed the team. There are also analysts with valuable skills that indirectly make the research successful.

Publishers are therefore creating forms for entering author information that specifies the role each author played, called multidimensional author descriptions. Data mining can produce measures of how many papers each author has worked on and the relative influence of each. Universities and companies can use these insights to hire good candidates to fill the particular skills they need.

One of the first steps to data sharing is simply to identify and label it, at the relevant granularity. For scientific data, one linchpin is the Digital Object Identifier (DOI) (*http://bit.ly/1dpxta5*), which uniquely identifies each data set. When creating a DOI, a researcher provides critical metainformation, such as contact information and when the data was created. Other researchers can then retrieve this information and use it when determining whether to use the data set, as well as to cite the original researcher. Metrics can determine the *impact factor* of a data set, as they now do for journals (*http://tmsnrt.rs/1al83A7*).

Sage supports DOIs and is working on a version layer, so that if data changes, a researcher can gain access both to the original data set and the newer ones. Clearly, it's important to get the original data set if one wants to reproduce an experiment's result. Versioning allows a data set to keep up with advances, just as it does for source code.

Stephen Friend, founder of Sage, said in his opening remarks that the field needs to move from hypothesis-driven data analysis to data-driven data analysis. He highlighted funders as the key force who can drive this change, which affects the recruitment of patients, the collection and storage of data, and collaboration of teams around the globe. Meanwhile, Sage has intervened surgically to provide tools and bring together the people that can make this shift happen.

Making Government Health Data Personal Again

An interview with Fred Smith of the CDC on their open content APIs.

By Julie Steele (*http://bit.ly/1al7dTK*)

Health care data liquidity (the ability of data to move freely and securely through the system) is an increasingly crucial topic in the era of big data. Most conversations about data liquidity focus on patient data, but other kinds of information need to be able to move freely and securely, too. Enter several government initiatives, including efforts at agencies within the Department of Health and Human Services (HHS (*http://1.usa.gov/1al83Qy*)) to make their content more easily available.

Fred Smith is team lead for the Interactive Media Technology Team in the Division of News and Electronic Media in the Office of the Associate Director for Communication for the U.S. Centers for Disease Control and Prevention (*http://1.usa.gov/1dpxwmj*) (CDC) in Atlanta. We recently spoke by phone to discuss ways in which the CDC is working to make their information more "liquid": easier to access, easier to repurpose, and easier to combine with other data sources.

Which data is available from the CDC APIs?

Fred Smith: In essence, what we're doing is taking our unstructured web content and turning it into a structured database, so we can call an API into it for reuse. It's making our content available (*http://1.usa.gov/1al846X*) for our partners to build into their websites or applications or whatever they're building.

Todd Park (*http://1.usa.gov/1dpxz1s*) likes to talk about "liberating data"–well, this is liberating content. What is a more high-value data set than our own public health messaging? It incorporates not only HTML-based text, but also we're building this to include multimedia —whether it's podcasts, images, web badges, or other content—and have all that content be aware of other content based on category or *taxonomy*. So it will be easy to query, for example: "What content does the CDC have on smoking prevention?"

Let's say there was a survey on youth tobacco use. Instead of saying, "Congratulations, here's 678,000 rows of the data set," we can say, "Here's the important message that you can use in your state about what teens are doing in your particular area of the country." We're distilling information down to useful messages or relevant data visualizations, and then pointing back to the open data sets.

You mentioned making content available for your partners. Who are they?

Fred Smith: It's a combination of other government health agencies, like other agencies inside HHS (*http://1.usa.gov/1al83Qy*), such as FDA (*http://1.usa.gov/1dpxzhR*) [the Food and Drug Administration] or NIH (*http://1.usa.gov/1al84E7*) [National Institutes of Health], other federal agencies like VA (*http://1.usa.gov/1dpxx9P*) [the Department of Veterans Affairs] or DOD [Department of Defense], the state and local health departments, universities, hospitals, nonprofit organizations like the American Cancer Society or the American Heart Association, or other public health nonprofits.

What do you hope people will do with the content?

Fred Smith: Communication hinges on knowing one's audience. On the federal level, we have an understanding of the country as a whole. But in a given state or county, they may know that certain messages work better. So by enabling these credible, scientific messages to be reused, the people who are building products and might know their micro-audience better than we do can get the benefit of using evidence-based messaging tailored for their audiences.

For example, say that a junior in a high school somewhere in Nebraska has started to learn web programming and APIs, and wants to write an application that she knows will help students in her high school avoid smoking. She can build something with their high school colors or logo, but fill it with our scientific content. It helps the information to improve people's health to go down to a local level and achieve something the government couldn't achieve on its own.

We took my daughter into the pediatrician a number of years ago, and the doctor was telling us about her condition, but it was something I'd never heard of before. She said, "Just a moment…" and went to the computer and printed off something from *cdc.gov* and handed it to me. My first reaction was, "Whew, my baby's going to be okay." My second was, "Ooo, that's the old web template." My third was, "If that had been flowed into a custom template from my doctor's office, I would have felt a lot more like my doctor knows what's going on, even if the information itself came from CDC." People trust their health care providers, and that's something we want to leverage.

It seems that you're targeting a broad spectrum of developers here, rather than scientists or researchers. Why that choice of audience?

Fred Smith: The scientific community and researchers already know about CDC and our data sets, and how to get hold of them. So just exposing the data isn't the issue. The issue is more: how can we expand the impact of these data? Going back to the digital government strategy (*http://1.usa.gov/1al84UG*), the reason that the federal government is starting to focus on opening these data sets, opening APIs, and going more mobile, is to increase our offering of citizen services toward the end of getting the information and what it all means out to the public better.

It's a question of transparency, but throwing open the data is only part of it. Very few people really want to spend time analyzing a two-million-row data set.

Are you finding any resistance to echoing government messaging, or are people generally happy to redistribute the content?

Fred Smith: We're fortunate at the CDC that we have strong brand recognition and are considered very trustworthy and credible, and that's obviously what we strive for. We sometimes get push-back, but generally our partners like to use the information and they were going to reuse it anyway; this just gives them a mechanism to use it more easily.

We work with a lot of state and local health departments, and when there's some kind of outbreak—for example, SARS—we often start out with a single page. SARS was new and emerging to the entire world, the CDC included. We were investigating rapidly, and in the course of a few days, we went from one page to dozens or more; our website (*http://1.usa.gov/1dpxxGI*) was constantly being updated. But we've got these public health partners who are not geared up for 24/7/365 operations the way we are. The best they could do was link out to us and hope that their visitors followed those links. In some cases, they copied and pasted, but they couldn't keep up with events. So, allowing this API into the content—so they can use our JavaScript widget—means that they get to make sure that their content stays up to date and their recommendations stay current.

How is this project related to the Blue Button (*http://1.usa.gov/1al85b7*) initiative, if at all?

Fred Smith: It's not, really. That's focused on an EHR [electronic health record], and health records are essentially doctors' notes written for other doctors; they are not necessarily notes written out to the patient. Content services or content syndication could be leveraged to put a little context around that health record. For example, someone could write an application so that when you downloaded the data from the Blue Button, unknown terms could be looked up and linked from the National Library of Medicine. It could supplement your health record with the science and suggestions from the CDC and other parts of HHS. We think it would be a great add-on.

What data might be added to the API in the near future?

Fred Smith: The multimedia part will be added in the next 8–10 months. CDC has a number of data sets that are already publicly available, but many of them don't yet have a RESTful API into them yet, particularly some of the smaller databases. So we're looking at what we can open up.

And we're not only doing this here at CDC. This idea of opening up a standard API into our content, including multimedia, is a joint effort among several agencies within HHS. We're in varying stages of getting content into these, but we're working to make this system interchangeable so this content can flow more easily from place to place. Most people don't care how the federal government is organized or what the difference in mission is between NIH and CDC, for example. The more we can use these APIs to break down some of those content silos, the better it is for us and for the general public.

We're excited about that, and excited that this core engine is an open source project—we've released it to SourceForge (*http://bit.ly/1dpxAlT*). A lot of our mobile apps use this same API, and we'll be releasing the base code for those products as well in the next couple of months.

Driven to Distraction: How Veterans Affairs Uses Monitoring Technology to Help Returning Veterans

Fujitsu provides the Sprout device to collect and analyze sensor data in real time

By Andy Oram (*http://bit.ly/1al6d2a*)

Veterans Affairs is collaborating with Fujitsu on a complex and interesting use of sensor data to help rehabilitate veterans suffering from post traumatic stress disorder (PTSD). I recently talked about this initiative with Dr. Steven Woodward, Principal Investigator of the study at the VA Palo Alto Health Care System, and with Dr. Ajay Chander, Senior Researcher in Data Driven Health Care at Fujitsu Laboratories of America (FLA).

The study is focused on evaluating strategies for driving rehabilitation. During deployments, veterans adapt their driving behavior to survive in dangerous war zones that are laced with combat fire, ambushes, and the threat of improvised explosive devices. Among veterans suffering from PTSD, these behaviors are hard to unlearn upon their return from such deployments. For example, some veterans veer instinctively into the middle of the road, reacting to deep-seated fears of improvised explosive devices. Others refuse to stop at stop signs for fear of attack. Other risky behaviors range from road rage to scanning the sides of the road instead of focusing on the road ahead. At-fault accident rates are significantly higher for veterans upon return from a deployment than before it.

The VA's research objective is to understand the triggers for PTSD and discover remedies that will enable veterans to return to normal life. For the study, the VA instrumented a car as well as its veteran driver with a variety of sensors that collect data on how the car is being driven and the driver's physiology while driving it. These sensors included wireless accelerometers on the brake and accelerator pedals and on the steering wheel, a GPS system, and an EKG monitor placed on the driver and wired to an in-car laptop for real-time viewing of cardiological signals, as well as manual recording of the driver's state and environmental cues by an in-car psychotherapist. With such a system, the VA's goal was to record and analyze driving trails of veterans and assess the efficacy of driving rehabilitation techniques.

As Dr. Woodward explained, the VA had been assessing veterans' driving habits for quite a while before getting introduced to Fujitsu's real-time monitoring technology. Assessments had been a significant challenge for multiple reasons. On the data collection and visualization front, the disparate sensors, the laptop, and the power supplies added up to a significant in-car IT footprint. More importantly, since all sensor systems were manufactured by different vendors and didn't share data with each other, the data streams were not synchronized. This made it difficult for the VA researchers to get an accurate understanding of how the driver's physiology coupled with the car's drive and location data.

Fujitsu Labs' Sprout device has allowed the VA researchers to address both issues. The Sprout, which runs Linux 3.0, collects data from multiple sensors in real time, time synchronizes and stores the data, and runs applications that analyze the data in real time. The Sprout is designed for mobile data collection and analysis: it runs off a battery, and is smaller than a pack of cards. It is general purpose in that it can support any sensor that speaks Bluetooth or WiFi and provides a general API for building real-time applications that use multisensor data.

Body sensors on a Zephyr chest strap (*http://bit.ly/1dpxACt*) measure EKG, heart rate, respiration, and other physiological data from the veteran driver. Accelerometers on iOS devices are used to capture pedal and steering wheel motion. An iPhone collects GPS location, and is used by the in-car therapist to record driving and environmental events by choosing them from a pre-populated list.

All these sensors send their data continuously over Bluetooth and WiFi to the in-car Sprout, which synchronizes and stores them. The Sprout then makes this data available to an iPhone application that visualizes it in real time for the in-car therapist. After the drive, VA researchers have been able to easily correlate all these data streams because they are all time synchronized. So far, more than 10 veterans have gone on more than 25 drives using this new infrastructure.

Fujitsu anticipates that many applications of its real-time monitoring and analysis platform will emerge as more sensors are integrated and new services are built on top of it. Some of these applications include:

- Monitoring health, rehabilitation, medication adherence, and well being in a patient-centered medical home
- Tracking workers on assembly lines to enhance safety and discover system-wide troublesome hotspots
- Monitoring call center phone operators in order to route calls to the least stressed operator
- Monitoring workers in high-risk jobs, such as train drivers

"As we become more digitally readable through increasingly cheaper and ubiquitous sensors, algorithms will afford us greater awareness of our own selves and advice on living and navigating our lives well," wrote Dr. Chander.

Growth of SMART Health Care Apps May Be Slow, but Inevitable

Harvard Medical School conference lays out uses for a health data platform

By Andy Oram (*http://bit.ly/1al6d2a*)

This week has been teeming with health care conferences, particularly in Boston, and was declared by President Obama to be National Health

IT Week (*http://bit.ly/1dpxASU*) as well. I chose to spend my time at the second ITdotHealth conference (*http://bit.ly/1al85YO*), where I enjoyed many intense conversations with some of the leaders in the health care field, along with news about the SMART Platform (*http://bit.ly/1dpxB9D*) at the center of the conference, the excitement of a Clayton Christensen talk, and the general panache of hanging out at the Harvard Medical School.

SMART, funded by the Office of the National Coordinator (ONC) in Health and Human Services, is an attempt to slice through the Babel of EHR formats that prevents useful applications from being developed for patient data. Imagine if something like the wealth of mashups built on Google Maps (crime sites, disaster markers, restaurant locations) existed for your own health data. This is what SMART hopes to do. They can already showcase some working apps, such as overviews of patient data for doctors, and a real-life implementation of the heart disease user interface (*http://wrd.cm/1al88DZ*) proposed by David McCandless in *Wired* magazine.

The Premise and Promise of SMART

At this conference, the presentation that gave me the most far-reaching sense of what SMART can do was by Nich Wattanasin, project manager for i2b2 at Partners. His implementation showed SMART not just as an enabler of individual apps, but as an environment where a user could choose the proper app for his immediate needs. For instance, a doctor could use an app to search for patients in the database matching certain characteristics, then select a particular patient and choose an app that exposes certain clinical information on that patient. In this way, SMART can combine the power of many different apps that had been developed in an uncoordinated fashion, and make a comprehensive data analysis platform from them.

Another illustration of the value of SMART came from lead architect Josh Mandel. He pointed out that knowing a child's blood pressure means little until one runs it through a formula based on the child's height and age. Current EHRs can show you the blood pressure reading, but none does the calculation that shows you whether it's normal or dangerous. A SMART app has been developed to do that. (Another speaker claimed that current EHRs in general neglect the special requirements of child patients.)

SMART is a close companion to the Indivo patient health record (*http://bit.ly/1dpxCtW*). Both of these, along with the i2b2 (*http://bit.ly/1al86vJ*) data exchange system, were covered in an article from an earlier conference at the medical school (*http://bit.ly/1dpxESB*). Let's see where platforms for health apps are headed.

How Far We've Come

As I mentioned, this ITdotHealth conference was the second to be held. The first took place in September 2009, and people following health care closely can be encouraged by reading the notes from that earlier instantiation of the discussion (*http://bit.ly/1al89aI*).

In September 2009, the HITECH act (part of the American Recovery and Reinvestment Act) defined the concept of *meaningful use*, but nobody really knew what was expected of health care providers, because the ONC and the Centers for Medicare and Medicaid Services did not release their final Stage 1 rules until more than a year after this conference. Aneesh Chopra, then the Federal CTO, and Todd Park, then the CTO of Health and Human Services, spoke at the conference, but their discussion of health care reform was a "vision." A surprisingly strong statement for patient access to health records was made, but speakers expected it to be accomplished through the CONNECT Gateway (*http://bit.ly/1dpxD14*), because there was no Direct. (The first message I could find on the Direct Project forum dated back to November 25, 2009 (*http://bit.ly/1al89aY*).) Participants had a sophisticated view of EHRs as platforms for applications, but SMART was just a "conceptual framework (*http://bit.ly/1dpxDhN*)."

So in some ways, ONC, Harvard, and many other contributors to modern health care have accomplished an admirable amount over three short years. But some ways we are frustratingly stuck. For instance, few EHR vendors offer API access to patient records, and existing APIs are proprietary. The only SMART implementation for a commercial EHR mentioned at this week's conference was one created on top of the Cerner API by outsiders (although Cerner was cooperative). Jim Hansen of Dossia (*http://bit.ly/1al89HN*) told me that there is little point to encourage programmers to create SMART apps while the records are still behind firewalls.

Keynotes

I couldn't call a report on ITdotHealth complete without an account of the two keynotes by Christensen and Eric Horvitz, although these took off in different directions from the rest of the conference and served as hints of future developments.

Christensen is still adding new twists to the theories laid out in *The Innovator's Dilemma* and other books. He has been a backer of the SMART project from the start and spoke at the first ITdotHealth conference. Consistent with his famous theory of disruption, he dismisses hopes that we can reduce costs by reforming the current system of hospitals and clinics. Instead, he projects the way forward through technologies that will enable less trained experts to successively take over tasks that used to be performed in more high-cost settings. Thus, nurse practitioners will be able to do more and more of what doctors do, primary care physicians will do more of what we current delegate to specialists, and ultimately the patients and their families will treat themselves.

He also has a theory about the progression toward openness. Radically new technologies start out tightly integrated, and because they benefit from this integration they tend to be created by proprietary companies with high profit margins. As the industry comes to understand the products better, they move toward modular, open standards and become commoditized. Although one might conclude that EHRs, which have been around for some forty years, are overripe for open solutions, I'm not sure we're ready for that yet. That's because the problems the health care field needs to solve are quite different from the ones current EHRs solve. SMART is an open solution all around, but it could serve a marketplace of proprietary solutions and reward some of the venture capitalists pushing health care apps (*http://oreil.ly/1dpxDOA*).

While Christensen laid out the broad environment for change in health care, Horvitz gave us a glimpse of what he hopes the practice of medicine will be in a few years. A distinguished scientist at Microsoft, Horvitz has been using machine learning to extract patterns in sets of patient data. For instance, in a collection of data about equipment uses, ICD codes, vital signs, etc., from 300,000 emergency room visits, they found some variables that predicted a re-admission within 14 days. Out of 10,000 variables, they found 500 that were relevant, but because the relational database was strained by retrieving so much data, they reduced the set to 23 variables to roll out as a product.

Another project predicted the likelihood of medical errors from patient states and management actions. This was meant to address a study claiming that most medical errors go unreported.

A study that would make the privacy-conscious squirm was based on the willingness of individuals to provide location data to researchers. The researchers tracked searches on Bing along with visits to hospitals and found out how long it took between searching for information on a health condition and actually going to do something about it. (Horvitz assured us that personally identifiable information was stripped out.)

His goal is to go beyond measuring known variables, and to find new ones that could be hidden causes. But he warned that, as is often the case, causality is hard to prove.

As prediction turns up patterns, the data could become a *fabric* on which many different apps are based. Although Horvitz didn't talk about combining data sets from different researchers, it's clearly suggested by this progression. But proper de-identification and flexible patient consent become necessities for data combination. Horvitz also hopes to move from predictions to decisions, which he says is needed to truly move to evidence-based health care.

Did the Conference Promote More Application Development?

My impression (I have to admit I didn't check with Dr. Ken Mandl, the organizer of the conference) was that this ITdotHealth aimed to persuade more people to write SMART apps, provide platforms that expose data through SMART, and contribute to the SMART project in general. I saw a few potential app developers at the conference, and a good number of people with their hands on data who were considering the use of SMART. I think they came away favorably impressed–maybe by the presentations, maybe by conversations that the meeting allowed them to have with SMART developers–so we may see SMART in wider use soon. Participants came far for the conference; I talked to one from Geneva, for instance.

The presentations were honest enough, though, to show that SMART development is not for the fainthearted. On the supply side—that is, for people who have patient data and want to expose it—you have to create a *container* that presents data in the format expected by SMART.

Furthermore, you must make sure the data conforms to industry standards, such as SNOMED for diagnoses. This could be a lot of conversion.

On the application side, you may have to deal with SMART's penchant for Semantic Web technologies such as OWL and SPARQL. This will scare away a number of developers. However, speakers who presented SMART apps at the conference said development was fairly easy. No one matched the developer who said their app was ported in two days (most of which were spent reading the documentation) but development times could usually be measured in months.

Mandl spent some time airing the idea of a consortium to direct SMART. It could offer conformance tests (but probably not certification, which is a heavyweight endeavor) and interact with the ONC and standards bodies.

After attending two conferences on SMART, I've got the impression that one of its most powerful concepts is that of an "app store for health care applications." But correspondingly, one of the main sticking points is the difficulty of developing such an app store. No one seems to be taking it on. Perhaps SMART adoption is still at too early a stage.

Once again, we are banging our heads up against the walls erected by EHRs to keep data from being extracted for useful analysis. And behind this stands the resistance of providers, the users of EHRs, to give their data to their patients or to researchers. This theme dominated a federal government conference on patient access (*http://oreil.ly/1al87jc*).

I think SMART will be more widely adopted over time because it is the only useful standard for exposing patient data to applications, and innovation in health care demands these apps. Accountable care organizations, smarter clinical trials (I met two representatives of pharmaceutical companies at the conference), and other advances in health care require data crunching, so those apps need to be written. And that's why people came from as far as Geneva to check out SMART—there's nowhere else to find what they need. The technical requirements to understand SMART seem to be within the developers' grasps.

But a formidable phalanx of resistance remains, from those who don't see the value of data to those who want to stick to limited exchange formats such as CCDs. And as Sean Nolan of Microsoft pointed out, one doesn't get very far unless the app can fit into a doctor's existing workflow. Privacy issues were also raised at the conference, because patient fears could stymie attempts at sharing. Given all these impediments, the government is doing what it can; perhaps the marketplace will step in to reward those who choose a flexible software platform for innovation.

Quantified Self to Essential Self: Mind and Body as Partners in Health

A movement to bring us into a more harmonious relationship with our bodymind and with technology.

By Linda Stone (*http://oreil.ly/1dpxGdl*)

"What are you tracking?" This is the conversation at quantified self (QS) meetups. The quantified self movement celebrates "self-knowledge through numbers." In our current love affair with QS, we tend to focus on data and the mind. Technology helps manage and mediate that relationship. The body is in there somewhere, too, as a sort of *slave* to the mind and the technology.

From blood sugar to pulse, from keystrokes to time spent online, the assumption is that there's power in numbers. We also assume that what can be measured is what matters, and if behaviors can be measured, they can be improved. The entire quantified self movement has grown around the belief that numbers give us an insight into our bodies that our emotions don't have.

However, in our relationship with technology, we easily fall out of touch with our bodies. We know how many screen hours we've logged, but we are less likely to be able to answer the question: "How do you feel?"

In our obsession with numbers and tracking, are we moving further and further away from the wisdom of the body? Our feelings? Our senses? Most animals rely entirely on their senses and the wisdom of the body to inform their behavior. Does our focus on numbers, measuring, and tracking move us further and further away from cultivating a real connection to our *essential self*?

What if we could start a movement that addresses our sense of self and brings us into a more harmonious relationship with our bodymind and with technology? This new movement would co-exist alongside the quantified self movement. I'd like to call this movement the *essential self* movement.

This isn't an either/or proposition–QS and essential self movements both offer value. The question is: in what contexts are the numbers more helpful than our senses? In what constructive ways can technology speak more directly to our bodymind and our senses?

I've always enjoyed "the numbers" when I'm healthy, and this probably has contributed to making good health even better. When I'm not healthy, the numbers are like cudgels, contributing to a feeling of hopelessness and despair.

For people struggling with health challenges, taking medication as directed can be considered a significant accomplishment. Now, progressive health clinics are asking diabetics to track blood sugar, exercise, food intake, and more. While all of this *is* useful information, the thing not being tracked is what high or low blood sugar *feels* like, or what it *feels* like to be hungry or full. The factors contributing to the numbers often are not and cannot easily be recorded.

I love the IBGStar (*http://bit.ly/1al89Yq*) for measuring blood sugar. For me, the most helpful information is in all the information around what might have contributed to the numbers: how late did I eat dinner? How many hours did I sleep? Did I eat a super large meal? Did I exercise after dinner? Did I *feel* that my blood sugar was high or low? What did that feel like? Tracking answers to these questions touches on elements of both QS and essential self.

So, what is essential self and what technologies might we develop? The essential self is that pure sense of presence—the "I am." The essential self is about our connection with our essential nature. The physical body, our senses and feelings are often responsive to our behaviors, to others, and to activities in ways to which we fail to attend. What if we cultivated our capacity to tune in in the same way animals tune in? What if we had a set of supportive technologies that could help us tune in to our essential self?

Passive, ambient, noninvasive technologies are emerging as tools to help support our essential self. Some of these technologies work with light, music, or vibration to support *flow-like* states. We can use these technologies as *prosthetics for feeling* (using them is about experiencing versus tracking). Some technologies support more optimal breathing practices. Essential Self technologies might connect us more directly to our limbic system, bypassing the *thinking mind*, to support our essential self.

When data and tracking take center stage, the thinking mind is in charge. And, as a friend of mine says, "I used to think my mind was the best part of me. Then I realized what was telling me that."

Here are a few examples of outstanding essential self technologies:

JustGetFlux.com (*http://bit.ly/1dpxGtT*) More than eight million people have downloaded f.lux. Once downloaded, f.lux matches the light from the computer display to the time of day: warm at night and like sunlight during the day. The body's circadian system is sensitive to blue light, and f.lux removes most of this stimulating light just before you go to bed. These light shifts are more in keeping with your circadian rhythms and might contribute to better sleep and greater ease in working in front of the screen. This is easy to download, and once installed, requires no further action from you—it manages the display light passively, ambiently, and noninvasively.

Focusatwill.com (*http://bit.ly/1al87Qg*) When neuroscience, music, and technology come together brilliantly, *focusatwill.com* is the result. Many of us enjoy listening to music while we work. The folks at *focusatwill.com* understand which music best supports sustained, engaged attention, and have curated a music library that can increase attention span up to 400% according to their website. The selections draw from core neuroscience insights to subtly and periodically change the music so your brain remains in a *zone* of focused attention without being distracted. *Attention amplifying* music soothes and supports sustained periods of relaxed focus. I'm addicted.

Heartmath EmWave2 (*http://bit.ly/1dpxJFW*) Just for fun, use a Heartmath EmWave2 to track the state of your autonomic nervous system while you're listening to one of the *focusatwill.com* music channels.